For a preview of upcoming books and information about the author, visit JamesPatterson.com or find him on Facebook, X, Instagram, or Substack.

# THE
# #1 DAD
# BOOK

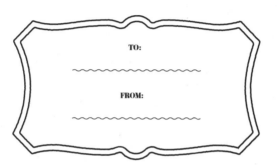

TO:

~~~~~~~~~~~~~~~~~~~~~~~~

FROM:

~~~~~~~~~~~~~~~~~~~~~~~~

# THE #1 DAD BOOK

## BE THE <u>BEST DAD</u>
### YOU CAN BE—
## <u>IN 1 HOUR!</u>

## James Patterson

LITTLE, BROWN AND COMPANY
*New York Boston London*

Little, Brown and Company
Hachette Book Group
1290 Avenue of the Americas, New York, NY 10104
littlebrown.com

First Edition: May 2025

Little, Brown and Company is a division of Hachette Book Group, Inc.
The Little, Brown name and logo are trademarks of Hachette Book Group, Inc.

The publisher is not responsible for websites (or their content)
that are not owned by the publisher.

The Hachette Speakers Bureau provides a wide range of authors for speaking
events. To find out more, go to hachettespeakersbureau.com or email
hachettespeakers@hbgusa.com.

Little, Brown and Company books may be purchased in bulk for business,
educational, or promotional use. For information, please contact your local
bookseller or the Hachette Book Group Special Markets Department at
special.markets@hbgusa.com.

Book interior design by Jeff Stiefel

ISBN 9780316585071
LCCN 2025930857

Printing 1, 2025

LSC-C

Printed in the United States of America

# THE
# #1 DAD
# BOOK

The Most

Important

Thing You'll

Ever Do

Is Be

the Best Dad

You Can Be

**H**ey, dad.

(Or soon-to-be dad.)

I get it.

You're busy as a beaver in flood times. Busy as popcorn in a skillet.

You're distracted.

You're under pressures people don't always understand.

You don't have time for…well, lots of things you'd like to have time for.

You're frustrated at times.

Just the other day, you couldn't find the car keys, or your wallet, or the TV remote.

Or all of the above.

Occasionally, you can be a knucklehead.

That's okay.

This batshit crazy world isn't making things any easier.

It's like the title of that old show from Broadway: *Stop the World—I Want to Get Off.*

You can't get off this not-so-merry-go-round, though.

But you do love your kids (or kid) more than anything.

You want them to have really good lives.

You're doing the best you can.

But you know what? *You can do better.*

Yeah, you can.

These pages can help.

It'll be quick…and mostly painless.

And it *will* make you a better dad.

Even if just two, or three, or five of these ideas work for you.

You'll be a better dad. Maybe a whole lot better.

And that'll be a good thing for everybody you care about.

Especially your kids.

I did the homework, so you don't have to do as much. I talked to lots of experts, and lots of dads, and lots of experts who are also dads. I read everything I could. Then I wrote and rewrote this book.

The pro-football coach Bill Parcells once said, "You are what your record says you are."

Your kids are *your* record.

So, turn the page, dad.

You're in.

You just made a big commitment.

One hour.

# Operating
# Instructions
# (For This Book,
# Not Your Kids)

**D**on't be afraid to mark up these pages with a sawed-off pencil or a pen subversively leaking ink.

Or use crayons. Or colored pencils. Go wild. Underline or highlight anything that makes sense to you.

This is going to work, big guy.

It's like a writer friend of mine told me, "Once a really good idea gets inside your head, it's impossible to get it out."

And there are some good ideas here, I promise!

Put a big fat check mark next to the ones that sound right to you—those are the things you *know* you can do to get better as a pop.

*On the flip side, some of these tips might feel all wrong to you.* Or to your partner. They might even seem stupid. Or simplistic. Or too politically correct. Or too politically incorrect.

Cross out anything and everything you *don't* agree with! Be aggressive with those ~~cross outs~~!

The job here—success—is to get better. Just making this one-hour commitment is a good start.

When you think about it, becoming a better dad is like anything else you've learned to get better at. You've probably figured out how to get better at some sport. Maybe you've learned to cook. Or at least grill. You've learned how to get better at your job.

You practiced. You concentrated. And you got better. Maybe a lot better.

So, you've done this before.

The ESPN host Dick Schaap said there were only two kinds of teams.

The ones filled with people trying to make the world dumber. And the ones filled with people trying to smarten it up.

Be a smarten-upper.

You can even make up dumb words like *smarten-upper*.

~~~~~~ 66 ~~~~~~

"I realized what fatherhood really
meant when our first child, our son,
was born and he was unable to breathe.
I felt a surge of anguish and terror
and grief because it was so wrong that
he would have never been fully alive
before he could simply disappear.
That's something like the awakening
I think every father feels at some time
in his life. Our son recovered, grew up,
and he's an absolutely great guy."

—BILL, JOURNALIST; ONE DAUGHTER, ONE SON

Here's to

New Dads—

and Old Vets

**M**aybe you're a newbie. Or maybe you're becoming a dad again. Whatever kind of dad you are, congrats! You're part of a sacred brotherhood. And a fatherhood. A very long line of dads. At times, that can be very comforting.

You're not alone.

First, you need to know this: After the baby is born, everybody will be mostly fussing over mom and the baby, not you. That's natural. It's totally fair.

Pregnancy is an unbelievably tough gig. You have no idea. Me neither.

And babies have their own adorable ways of demanding attention.

But what about the dad?

After the baby comes, dads need some hugs too. Dads need the occasional "attaboy."

Because pregnancy is hard for the dad too.

There, I said it. Out loud.

Mom, if you're reading this, go ahead and throw this very nice book (that you probably bought) at the nearest wall.

But show dad some compassion. He's not as smart as you.

And everything just changed for him too.

"Like so much between fathers
and sons, playing catch was tender
and tense at the same time."

—DONALD HALL, POET; ONE DAUGHTER, ONE SON

# Name Calling

Okay, so what are you going to name your new human? That's a very good topic for your babymoon. (Some couples take a trip before the baby is born. It's called a babymoon. Didn't take one myself, but it sounds like a cool idea.)

This is one of your first dad jobs. And it's a big one. Talk it over with your partner. Sleep on it. And don't take it lightly.

Here's a tip from a wise, helpful person: Before your baby is born, practice calling out the names you like at the dinner table a few dozen times. At the top of your lungs.

Which names sound best?

Which names are easiest to pronounce?

Which names get old really fast?

Remember, whatever name you choose, you're going to be calling it out many thousands of times over the next eighteen years. Make sure it rolls off your tongue.

Don't saddle your kid with a name that seems funny, or cute, or clever in the moment. Remember, it's not your name. It's the name your kid has to live with. Every day. For the rest of his or her life.

And not to get morbid, but someday it will be etched on a tombstone. *Here lies Mildred.* Or Ethel. Or Dick. Or Danger. Yes, some parents have named their child Danger.

Of course, that's not to say that kids can't make good with an unusual name.

Elvis made it work somehow.

So did Eldrick—though he's better known as Tiger.

Hopefully, so will Apple, a girl named after a very delicious fruit by her movie-star mom, Gwyneth Paltrow, and rock-star dad, Chris Martin.

My wife's dad's name was *Orville Berthold* Solie.

He decided he wanted to be called O.B.

Smart man.

O.B. became a very, very good dad.

He named his baby girl *Susan.*

~~~~~ 66 ~~~~~

"What brings us together is our love
of music. I'm from Jamaica, and we love
hip-hop. Sometimes my daughter and
I will go out on our own 'date' and that's
when we talk about *everything*.
At dinner, I'm not Daddy. I'm her friend.
Sometimes she says...'Forget you're my
dad...We're going to talk like friends.'
Becoming a dad taught me what love is.
I never really knew anything about love
until I became a dad."

—GESLEY, RESTAURANT MANAGER; ONE DAUGHTER

# Things Are
# About to
# Get Messy

know your time is valuable. I respect that. The one-hour clock is ticking.

We might as well get right into it.

Between your baby's birth and the end of toilet training, you'll be changing about eight thousand diapers. A lot of those diapers will be somewhere between foul and disgusting.

Get used to it.

Embrace the poop.

Laugh at the poop.

Talk to the poop.

*"Wow! How could so much poop come out of such a small person? This is impressive. Must be some kind of world record."*

Above all, don't put off dealing with the poop. Or the pee. You may not remember, but diaper rash really sucks. If it was your dirty underwear, you'd change it in a hurry, right?

It's not that hard. Just a little gross. Gross is no big deal.

So, roll up your sleeves, hold your breath, do your job.

Same goes for feeding time and bath time.

You're going to get sticky. You're going to get wet. So what? Dive right in.

Volunteer for service.

And remember this when you're at the supermarket. Seriously, don't mess up here. Baby wipes are essential for the health of your baby's behind. And for your mental health. And your partner's.

You can never have too many. Don't scrimp. Buy in bulk.

A lot of dad stuff is doing little things like that.

That's why it's easy to get better.

One mess at a time.

~~~~~~~~~ **66** ~~~~~~~~~

"The nature of impending
fatherhood is that you are
doing something that you're
unqualified to do."

—JOHN GREEN, AUTHOR; ONE SON, ONE DAUGHTER

~~~~ 66 ~~~~

"Our son is three. Fatherhood?
It's the best feeling in the world.
Puts a smile on my face early in the
morning. Gives me energy when
I'm tired. I want our boy to do
whatever makes him happy. But there's
such a thing as the family business.
If your father is a carpenter, you
probably know a little bit about wood.
If your father is a plumber, you know
something about pipes. I've been
involved with pro baseball all my life.
If he wants to play baseball, great.
If not, also great."

—CRAIG, BASEBALL SCOUT; ONE SON

Not a Hugger?

You Will Be

in a Minute

If there's one thing a lot of kid experts agree on, it's that human touch is life itself for babies. Remember, the little one just spent nine months *inside another body.* He or she craves contact.

Hold those little babies as much as you can.

Press them against your heart. They love to hear it thumping.

Hug them while they're awake. Hug them while they're sleeping.

They can't get enough of you.

Okay, sometimes they'll slime your favorite shirt. Or pants. Or even your ballcap. But that's a small price to pay.

And hugging isn't just for babies.

I have a good friend who raised a couple of football-playing boys. One Saturday night, the boys got up from the table after we all had dinner. They were about to walk out the front door when my friend called out to them: "Where do you two think you're going?"

The boys, big-time football players, came back and gave their dad a hug.

That scene taught me a lesson that I never forgot. More important, I've lived by it ever since.

Our son got a hug every morning when we dropped him off at school. We couldn't have cared less what the other kids thought. He felt the same way we did.

He's grown up now. But whenever he comes home, he still gets a hug.

He always will.

The author George Saunders said something that's been guiding me for the last couple of years.

It's this: "My time here is short—what can I do the most beautifully?"

One of the most beautiful things you can do is become a better father.

Starting with a hug.

~~~~~~ 66 ~~~~~~

"From the time our kids were very young, we would say, 'Let's do a big hug!' We'd put our arms around each other in a circle, draw in close, very close, and start saying in a quiet voice, 'AHHHH,' with eventual crescendos, *'AHHHH,'* until it was loud enough that we were all giggling. We still do it to this day."

—MARK, DOCTOR; TWO DAUGHTERS

~~~~~ 66 ~~~~~

"Be very loving, and by *loving*,
I mean not just caring for your
child—touching them, carrying them
when they're little, hugging them,
telling them you love them."

—JIM, CONSULTANT; THREE DAUGHTERS

~~~~~~~

"My father was not a hugger...not an
affection guy...He showed his love
in other ways...working hard...giving up
everything...My kids hug...They know
that I love them."

—DOUG, TEACHER; FOUR SONS

# You're One Big,

# Beautiful Noise

**B**y this point in your life, you've probably figured out that not everybody is in love with the sound of your voice.

But guess what? Your baby is.

It's a fact. Your voice is one of the greatest things he or she has ever heard.

So, sing to your baby. Even if you can't hold a tune.

Babies love rock 'n' roll. They love rap. They even like opera.

Talk to them before they can speak.

Once they start to talk, they'll have a lot of very smart questions.

Know why?

Because everything in the infinite number of universes is new to them.

So, try to answer their questions. Talk back in their alien tongue.

Teach them words from *your* alien language. Try not to teach them the f-word. Unless you want them using it in preschool.

Some studies show a father's vocabulary has a stronger effect on kids' language development than a mom's.

Okay, let's say it's a fifty-fifty thing, but play your part.

There will be days when you wish the terrible twos were far, far behind you.

Maybe put a check mark next to this one.

The ones and twos and threes will be over in the blink of an eye.

Gone girl. Gone boy.

Then what? Then you get old, dad. That happens in the blink of an eye too.

So, talk to your kids. Early and often.

And don't ever stop.

~~~~~~ 66 ~~~~~~

"I have a four-year-old and a teenager.
It's like, get ready to have all your
plans destroyed. The four-year-old talks
a lot. He's going to Christian school.
One day I told him to clean his room.
He said to me, 'Jesus is upset, and he
is going to come and put me in the
Thinking Chair.' The Thinking Chair
is what they call a time-out at the
Christian school. I tried not to laugh,
but he was so serious about it."

—ISRAEL, FILMMAKER; ONE SON, ONE STEPSON

# If You Read Nothing Else, Read This

**R**ead to your kids.
*You.*
*Read.*

It doesn't take much time to make a big difference.

Reading to your kids helps boost their brainpower.

It gives them new words and new ways of putting them together.

Think about this: Kids whose parents read to them daily are exposed to almost *three hundred thousand more words* before kindergarten than kids whose parents don't read to them.

That's more words than the first three Harry Potter books combined.

A pretty good head start going into school, right?

Reading to your kids exposes them to big emotions in stories and shows them that those feelings are normal.

(It's also a great time for you to ask questions like

"Have you ever felt like that?" or "What do you think would make Pooh feel better?")

Read to your kids until they're four or five.

Then flip things around. Let them read to you.

And don't just pick books that *you* think are good.

Find books that *they* think are good.

Let them see books in your house.

Here are some pretty cool books to read to your kids when they're little.

~~~~~~~~~~~~~~~~~~~~~~~~~~~~~~~~~~~~~~

*Be Glad Your Dad...(Is Not an Octopus!)* by Matthew Logelin and Sara Jensen, illustrated by Jared Chapman

It's always a bonus when kids get to learn something new and interesting while reading. This book gives kids lots of reasons to be glad their dad is who he is, and ends on fun facts about the animal dads featured in the story.

*I Am Every Good Thing* by Derrick Barnes, illustrated by Gordon C. James

This empowering ode to all the energy, goodness, and wonder in kids is also an ode to Black boyhood, and provides great affirmations to remind kids of their limitless potential.

*The Book with No Pictures* by B. J. Novak

A great read aloud for dads who love to be silly and make their kids laugh...and who don't mind saying "boo-boo butt" out loud.

*Because I'm Your Dad* by Ahmet Zappa, illustrated by Dan Santat

Nothing compares to the unconditional love a parent has for their child, and Ahmet Zappa (Frank Zappa's son) captures that perfectly here. The book is also silly and fun, making it another great read aloud.

~~~~~~~~~~~~~~~~~~~~~~~~~~

*Houdini and Me* by Dan Gutman

If you're looking for a novel to read together with an older kid, you can't go wrong picking a book by Dan Gutman. This one stars an eleven-year-old who is contacted by someone claiming to be Harry Houdini. There is great Houdini trivia, and plenty of action and twists to keep kids and adults turning the pages.

~~~~~~ 66 ~~~~~~

"It is easier to build strong children than to repair broken men."

—FREDERICK DOUGLASS, ABOLITIONIST LEADER; THREE SONS, TWO DAUGHTERS

# Be Consistent,

# Consistently

This is a biggie: Consistency builds trust. And trust is the foundation for just about everything that matters.

Be consistently fair with your kids.

Because your kids need to trust you.

They need to know you have their back.

You need to know they have your back.

Listening is incredibly important for building trust.

So is patience. And repetition.

Yep, *repetition.*

And never be afraid to say these three words to your kids, or your partner:

*I. Was. Wrong.*

*Consistent* doesn't mean boring. Here's a way to look at it.

Be consistently surprising. Good surprises take a little thought. Good surprises take a little planning.

Your kids might not always gush over your surprises at the time. Sometimes you'll wonder if they appreciate them at all.

Guess what? Years later, when you least expect it, they'll tell you how much those surprises meant.

It will happen. I promise.

Don't be surprised.

"I know a lot of single men and women who don't want to have children. Because it's work. Because it will change their lifestyle. But it's worth it. It's totally worth it. You don't know that until you hold your own child in your arms."

—JIM, CONSULTANT; THREE DAUGHTERS

# What's Your
# Story, Dude?

Here's another easy thing we can all do as dads.

Tell your kids your story. Make that your *stories*. Plural.

What do you value most? What's really important to you? What can't you live without? What *can* you live without?

Don't go on and on. Don't bore them to tears. Just tell them who you are, and more important, tell them what you stand for.

And then, let them tell you *their* stories.

Listen to your kids. Find out who they are. At their core.

If they're really not sure yet, if they're still struggling with it, help them to figure it out. It's hard. Remember how hard it was for you as a kid?

If the kids are already teens, or preteens, don't wait. Do it right away.

The idea is not to change your kids into who you are.

Or who you always wanted to be.

It's to help them discover who *they* are. Deep down inside.

Of course, once you open yourself up, your kids might also want to give you some free advice about yourself. That's a good thing.

It means they're interested. It means they care. And you'll be surprised at how much they've noticed about you.

Listen to their ideas about how you can get better. Don't be afraid to ask for help. That might be worth a check mark. In fact, I'll say it again:

*Don't be afraid to ask for help.*

Especially from your kids.

Nobody knows you better.

Here's a hard truth for me to tell: I think if I'd written this book before I had our son, I would've been a better dad.

~~~~~~~~~ 66 ~~~~~~~~~

"When our son was born, that week,
I started a journal of messages to him.
I wrote my last entry just before he
graduated from high school. I gave it to
him after graduation, and he didn't even
know that I had it. He started reading it
at our dinner table, and we were crying
and laughing at the same time."

—JEFF, EDUCATOR; ONE SON, ONE DAUGHTER

# Find Yourself
# Some Dad Buds

How many hours do you spend talking to other guys about work stuff? About fantasy football? About politics? About that balky sump pump in your basement?

Maybe, once in a while, try talking about dad stuff.

About what your kids are going through.

About what *you're* going through.

About your partner, and how they're doing.

Not every dad will be into it. Some of us need to play everything really close to the vest. No sharing.

But if you find a few who are willing to talk, you'll be amazed at how much you have in common, how much you can learn from one another, and how good it feels to share the load.

By the way, moms have been talking to one another like this for thousands of years. Maybe millions.

It's worked out pretty well.

~~~~~ 66 ~~~~~

"I've got a friend with four girls.
Three of them are teenagers.
He and I talk about our kids at least
once a week. We've become best friends
because of those talks. Our kids
are close too. And our wives."

—Neal, housepainter; two daughters, one son

Your Presence

Is Required

**H**ere's one of my trade secrets: When I'm writing a novel, I sometimes scrawl a note to myself at the top of a page that says, "Be there." It reminds me that I need to put the reader in the scene so that they'll really feel it.

The same goes for being a dad.

Let's be honest. There are lots of distractions in life. The Internet. Zoom calls with in-laws. Night shifts. Netflix. The NFL Draft.

There will be times when you can only give your kids part of your attention. But whenever you can, as much as you can, *focus*!

It's not just being around, although that's a big part of it. It's paying attention, setting other thoughts aside, and really being present. There are some woo-woo terms for this. *Intention. Mindfulness.* But what it comes down to is:

When you're with your kids, *be there.*

Have you ever seen little kids on a school stage lighting up when they spot their parents in the audience? It's like they're witnessing a miracle.

Now you're the miracle.

You might not be able to be at every recital, every birthday party, and every game.

But be at as many as you can.

It matters.

Sure, somebody else can shoot video of a game or birthday.

But it's only *live* once.

Years later, your kids will not remember what song they sang, what flavor cake they had, or whether they won or lost that third match of the season.

But they'll remember if you were there.

~~~~~~ **66** ~~~~~~

"Show up. You can't miss anything.

You gotta be there for them.

Your job can't get in the way, and it will.

When they tell you, 'It's okay, you don't

have to be there,' don't listen to them.

Just show up."

—BOB, TEACHER; TWO DAUGHTERS

# Old School

## vs.

# New School

## vs.

# You School

This is something a lot of dads struggle with. You don't have to be an old-school dad. Or a new-school dad.

Maybe the right thing is to take the best of both schools.

You do you.

No matter what you decide, good habits are hugely important.

What are some good habits that you can pass on to the kids?

And some bad habits that you can improve on—so that those bad habits *don't* get passed on?

You could make a list.

Unless that sounds stupid to you.

Then *don't* make a list.

But just in case you want to:

GOOD HABITS:

_____

_____

_____

_____

BAD HABITS:

_____

_____

_____

_____

I'll start.

Here's a good habit of mine. At least I think it's a good habit. I write every day. Seven days a week. And the thing is, I don't feel like I work for a living, I play for a living.

So that's probably a good habit.

Do I have bad habits? Yep. I eat too many hamburgers and drink too much soda.

And that's all you're getting out of me.

~~~~~~ **66** ~~~~~~

"I had a great father. He busted his ass.
He was a blue-collar teamster truck driver
for thirty-eight years. Back when I was a
kid, I was playing hockey. My brother was
on the same team. Our father was at the
game. There was a guy on the other
team really giving it to my brother.
A dirty player. So, I nailed him good.
During the fight, I was cursing. After the
game, my father came up to me, and I
could tell he was mad. He said he wasn't
upset because I defended my brother.
He said, 'Did you have to use such foul
language?' To this day, my dad is my role
model. Maybe now more than ever."

—JOE, COACH; TWO SONS

# Those Oldies
# but Goodies

**H**ere's some good news, dad. A rare win-win for you and the kids.

If your parents or those of your partner are around, you're blessed. Maybe twice blessed.

And so are your children.

Just build a relationship between your kids and your parents. Go with the flow. It will make you a better dad.

Most grandparents love their grandchildren. And grandchildren love their grandparents. So, you're starting from a position of strength.

Grandparents are from another generation. That can be a real plus. They experienced a very different world, and used life's tools that are almost unrecognizable today. "What is a type-writer?" "Black-and-white TV?" "Station wagons?" "You walked to school in the snow with no shoes?"

The positive side is that they can teach your kids a little history.

And give them some context about your family.

Maybe even an origin story or two.

They have stories to tell. Sometimes over and over.

But these are stories that will stay with your kids for the rest of their lives and maybe be passed on to your grandchildren.

They also knew relatives who aren't around anymore, but they're still part of your kids' DNA.

Some survived tragedy.

Some triumphed over adversity.

Some did small, everyday things that carry big lessons.

Some were just funny as hell.

Some of you might be saying, "I didn't exactly get along that well with my parents."

Well, get out of the way. This is about your kids. Your parents are probably different now, and the relationship between grandparents and grandchildren is definitely different than the one between you and your mom and dad.

Bonus!

Always remember this—grandparents are a great resource for free childcare and lots of cool presents.

~~~~~ 66 ~~~~~

"A few things in life are better
than advertised, and one of them is
being a grandparent. Grandchildren
are the greatest gift our daughter and
son-in-law could have possibly given to
us. Time with our grandchildren is
precious for my wife and me."

—BOB, ATTORNEY; ONE DAUGHTER, THREE GRANDKIDS

# The Incredible
# Power of No

Okay, remember that I'm just talking here. We're spending an hour together.

So, just for a minute, let's talk about saying no.

To your kids.

It can be a hard thing. But a good thing. A *necessary* thing.

People who know about this stuff say that dads who establish boundaries from the start are less likely to have kids with behavioral issues later.

And here's the secret that kids will never tell you: They actually *crave* boundaries. Boundaries help them feel safe.

It's not always easy. Kids are geniuses, diabolically clever about getting their way. And they will definitely test your limits. That's part of growing up.

But don't cave in when they throw temper tantrums or beg, or plead with those big, expressive eyes of theirs.

Don't reward bad behavior.

That's one of the most common mistakes we all make as parents.

Do not reward bad behavior.

And try to avoid anything that smacks of punishment for punishment's sake. Just because you're mad at them in the moment, don't take it out on them. You're the adult. You're the one they need to trust.

There have to be some rules in the house, right? Hopefully, not too many rules. And the rules need to be understood by everybody. They need to be fair. This isn't boot camp.

Here's one rule that fits all: When it's called for, you should absolutely say, "You can't talk to me or your mom like that."

That's a big no.

And the same goes for you when you're talking to your kids.

Words hurt.

Kindness counts.

And it goes both ways.

———～～～～ 66 ～～～～———

"Kids remember everything. Everything!
Just about everything you've ever said,
everything you've done. Things that
you've forgotten, they remind you
about twenty years later."

—JOHN, JOURNALIST; THREE DAUGHTERS

JAMES PATTERSON

~~~~~~ 66 ~~~~~~

"We were four boys.

We loved being around my dad.

We used to watch everything he did.

We would sit down and watch him eat.

And try to chew like him. The way he

walked. I said, 'That's the guy I want to

be when I grow up.' I was a screwup.

I probably shouldn't be in the police.

I was hanging around with the wrong

people. But I learned from my father.

He never, ever raised his hand, or even

his voice. He'd sit down and talk to you,

and you'd feel like you got your butt

whipped. But he never touched

any of us."

—CARLOS, DEPUTY POLICE CHIEF; ONE DAUGHTER

# Let's Take
# It Outside

**M**ost child psychologists—and most experienced dads—will back me up on this:

Never argue in front of the kids.

Especially *about* the kids.

They're watching. They're listening. They're learning.

The only time you should be raising your voice to your partner is when you're laughing your head off.

Or singing off-key.

Whatever issues or disagreements you're having, the two of you can talk it through later, one-on-one. No kids allowed.

If it can't wait, maybe go into the garage. Or out into the backyard. Or onto that nice little patio on the roof of your apartment building.

Whatever it takes, keep meanness out of your house.

You want meanness in your house even less than you want rodents.

Unless you just got suckered into having a pet hamster.

Rookie mistake.

When kids see parents argue, they get anxious. And when partners take opposite sides, kids get confused. And confusion breaks down trust.

Seeing parents argue is an opportunity that some kids will use to play you against each other. (They're clever that way.)

If your kids try to play the "but mom said" game, your response is simple.

"Well, let's go ask mom about that right now."

To get to mom, they've got to go through you, dad.

And vice versa.

Arguments between adult partners are natural and healthy.

But when the kids are around: United You Stand.

~~~~~~~~~ **❝** ~~~~~~~~~

"They see everything.

They hear everything...

They don't need a list of things they

need to be. They just need an example

of what to be. They need you. Being an

example shouldn't be 'Oh, I did this,'

or 'You should do that.' It's more subtle.

Kids read the room instantly."

—TERENCE, ATTORNEY; TWO SONS, ONE DAUGHTER

# Love Is in the Air (Or It Should Be)

Kids benefit from seeing their parents respecting each other and being affectionate with each other.

A little parental PDA can show them what a healthy, loving relationship looks like.

So let them see you holding hands.

Let them see you hug.

Let them see you kiss.

Let them hear you say, "I love you."

If you do it often enough, they'll learn not to chirp *ewww!* every time.

Now, some dads will say, "I'm not an 'I love you' kind of guy."

Says who? Who passed that law? Your dad? Your dad's dad?

You can be an "I love you" guy.

You can change. At least a little.

You'll be a better man for it.

Saying "I love you" is not a sign of weakness.
It's a sign of strength.
Now go ahead. Say "I love you."
Was that so hard?
If it was, say it again.
Okay, *I'll* say it. "I love you, man."

~~~~~~ **66** ~~~~~~

"My youngest has a rare disease
that affects his cognitive ability.
He decided to be one of the speakers
at his graduation. He's so shy and quiet
that we questioned his decision before
he went ahead with it. He gave this
incredibly humble speech of gratitude.
It was all about his school, his teachers,
and the other kids. The part that really
got us is that he broke down three times
while he was speaking. My son doesn't
cry. It was a beautiful thing to see
my child had grown into someone
so incredibly strong."

—SCOTT, TEACHER; THREE SONS

# My Bad

**G**uys, let's face it. We screw up a lot. I know I do. Sometimes, royally.

But here's the silver lining. That means we can be really, really good at teaching kids about resilience.

And how to confront challenges.

And deal with mistakes.

And *own* them.

Life isn't always fair. You already know that. But it's important that your kids learn it too. You don't have to be overly negative, or pessimistic, just realistic.

Muhammad Ali used to say, "There's nothing wrong with getting knocked down, as long as you get right back up."

Don't be afraid to discuss tough topics with your kids. They can take it.

Help them make good decisions.

Get them ready for the real world.

It's not getting any easier out there. To be honest, it seems to be getting harder every year.

You don't need to scare them. Just prepare them.

"We had this discussion a lot.
Sometimes you have to let them sink
to learn how to swim.
Don't be their life vest, not all the time—
you have to let them sink."

—STEVE, PHOTOGRAPHER; TWO DAUGHTERS

# Laugh It Off

With kids, a sense of humor is necessary for survival.

Yours and theirs.

When the going gets tough, sometimes the tough have to get funny. Sometimes the best thing you can do is laugh.

Be a goofball sometimes.

Adam Sandler meets Chris Rock. That's you.

Did you hear the one about the three stages for becoming a dad? First, you believe in Santa Claus. Then you don't believe in Santa Claus. Then you *are* Santa Claus.

Not that funny? So what? Try another joke.

Laugh at the situation.

Laugh at the problem.

Laugh at yourself. Hell, everybody else does.

Laughing releases tension.

It floods your brain with endorphins.

It's a bonding experience. The best possible kind.

The family that laughs together stays together.

~~~~~ 66 ~~~~~

"The thing about our meals together—
at home, at Mickey D's, wherever—
there're always laughs. Everybody thinks
they're the funniest ever. But I know
I'm the funniest. That's a joke."

—TED, CONSTRUCTION WORKER; TWO SONS, TWO DAUGHTERS

~~~~~~~

"My daughter is really cool. Really smart.
I'm kind of the clown in her world.
It's always, 'Dad, oh Dad.' She thinks
it's funny the way I dress, or the dance
moves I make, or the fact that I listen to
her music. The best advice I got from
another dad is, 'It only gets better;
you're going to get all this incredible
enrichment. Hang on tight.'"

—ANDREW, ASSISTANT MANAGER; ONE SON, ONE DAUGHTER

# The Good,
# the Bad,
# and the Boring

T here's no getting around it.

No matter how much you adore your kids, there will be times when dadhood is drudgery.

I'm not talking about changing diapers. Or rocking your little baby to sleep. We've covered all that.

I'm talking about later.

Like when your kid wants to watch the same Disney movie for the hundredth time.

Or when you have to pretend to love playing a video game that involves elves and magic coins.

Or when you have to be the Helping Dad at preschool.

That's hard time, my friend.

There will be days when you're convinced your brain is turning to mush. When you think you're losing your edge. When you feel like you've been reduced to a camp counselor, a babysitter, or a chauffeur. Or all three at once.

There will be times when you'll mutter—softly, to yourself—that you can't wait for the day to end.

But trust me on this—

There will come a time, not too far in the future, when you would pay a million dollars to have just one of those days back.

"My wife and I are both lucky.
We had good, loving parents guiding us.
So, we sort of inherited our parenting
skills. If you're lucky like that,
then emulate your parents."

—STEVE, PHOTOGRAPHER; TWO DAUGHTERS

~~~~~~~ 66 ~~~~~~~

"The process of living or working with children is demanding and exhausting. It requires heart, intelligence, and stamina. When we don't live up to our own expectations—and we won't always—let's be as kind to ourselves as we are to our youngsters. If our children deserve a thousand chances, and then one more, let's give ourselves a thousand chances—and then two more."

—ADELE FABER AND ELAINE MAZLISH,
*HOW TO TALK SO KIDS WILL LISTEN & LISTEN SO KIDS WILL TALK*

# The Magic
# of Rituals

**K**ids crave dependable patterns. Even if they don't know it. Even when they wouldn't admit it.

Schedule regular time with them. Don't just expect it to happen. *Make* it happen.

Be creative. Be a little clever. Be the charming guy you can be when you want to.

If you work from home these days, you have no excuses. Just start a little later once in a while. Or knock off a little early. Or block out some time on your schedule. It's as important as any meeting or deadline.

No. It's *more* important.

If you work in an office or a factory or a hospital or an Amazon warehouse, finding a regular time can be harder. Same for dads who drive trucks or manage farms or travel for a living.

But remember, it doesn't have to be a lot. It just

needs to be something your kids can count on. Something for them to look forward to. Something *consistent*. (See how that keeps coming back?)

Some families already have a lot of traditions. If you do, bring the kids in on them. Give them important roles.

If you don't have a lot of traditions, create some.

One of the simplest traditions starts around the table.

Whenever you can, eat meals as a family.

Some of the best conversations you will ever have will be at the dinner table with your kids.

What you'll remember most is their laughter.

Each one of those laughs is unique.

A thing unto itself.

A thing of beauty.

Definitely worth repeating.

~~~~~~~ **66** ~~~~~~~

"The most important thing is to get
your kids to talk to you. In our house,
I had this amnesty kind of thing.
We had this white bench in the front
yard, and I told the kids…when we're
sitting on this bench you can tell me
anything and it doesn't leave the bench.
I called it the B.T.…the Bench Talk. It was
a safe spot for me and the kids."

—ERIC, ATTORNEY; TWO DAUGHTERS

# The Lesson of

# the Five Balls

've always found this useful. I've pretty much lived by it.

Imagine life as a game in which you are juggling five balls in the air.

You name them—work, family, health, friends, and spirit—and you're keeping all of these in the air.

Hopefully, you will soon understand that work is a rubber ball. If you drop it, it will bounce back.

But the other four balls—family, health, friends, and spirit—are made of glass.

If you drop one of these, they will be irrevocably *scuffed, marked, nicked, damaged,* or even *shattered.* They will never be the same.

Once we understand that, maybe, just maybe, we will strive for more balance in our lives.

# Tattoo This
# Behind Your
# Eyeballs

W e're pals now, right?

So, you can take it when I give you some bad news.

Actually, you already know it, or at least you suspect it.

Let me break it to you as gently as I can:

It's time to grow the fuck up.

No more BASE jumping.

No more treks to Burning Man.

No more swimming with sharks.

If you're still smoking, or vaping, or chewing tobacco, now is the time to quit.

Ask yourself if you might be playing sports more often than you should. Like twice a week in your beer league. Followed by beers.

Or golfing both days on the weekend.

A few of my goofball friends, all dads, played in a men's basketball league into their mid-fifties. They had team jerseys that said Nobody Moves, Nobody Gets Hurt.

Unfortunately, they got hurt. A lot. Sprained ankles, broken fingers, dashed egos.

Do your family a favor. Take better care of yourself.

You might still feel like a kid.

But you're not.

You're a dad.

Try to stay off the injured list.

You're
the Man—
Live with It,
Live Up to It

You're (half) in charge of helping your kids take responsibility for their actions. If they did it, they need to own it. They do the crime, they do the time. (Hopefully, no real crimes.)

It starts with helping your kids understand the difference between right and wrong.

Sometimes, there are complicated, deep-rooted reasons why we make mistakes. Why we fail. But at some point, we have to take responsibility for our actions.

Help your kids. They're young. They're mostly innocent. They can be knuckleheads at times. But they do need to understand that actions have consequences.

Kids also need to understand that *character* means doing the right thing.

Even in an empty room, when nobody's watching.

Even if some people are getting away with doing the wrong thing. And they *are*.

Folks doing the wrong thing shouldn't be role models for our kids. But that's the case way too often. Especially on the Internet.

And that's where you come in, dad.

And not with too heavy a hand.

And not too often.

Just enough.

You've got the touch.

~~~~~~~~~~ **"** ~~~~~~~~~~

"My father was quiet and handsome,
an all-American running back in the
1940s. Eventually a football coach.
He was also very superstitious.
For years my brothers and I wondered
why he would never walk in front of a
parked car, always behind it.
Why would he never wear a seat belt?
Why he would whisper what seemed
a quick, quiet prayer before driving us
around as kids. When I got older, I finally
asked him about these silent quirks.
He told me as a Navy flier in the Pacific
he would pray before bombing runs and
tap his St. Christopher's medal. No seat
belt? He said too many guys he trained
with died, strapped in, trapped in

cockpits when their planes crash-landed, as his B-24 did on a remote Japanese island. Why avoid the front of a parked car? He recounted seeing airmen obliterated when they walked right into the invisible, spinning propellers of warplanes parked on hot, noisy flight lines...no doubt a horror he could never unsee. The idiosyncrasies and prayers that my brothers and I often joked about were his private release from experiences he kept to himself...likely for our sake. It wasn't weakness, or odd behavior. It was strength. That was his generation."

—TIM, JOURNALIST; NO KIDS

# Be Patient with Your Kids, with Your Partner, with Yourself

**M**ost good things don't happen all at once. That includes becoming a better dad. Improve one small thing at a time, then another, and another.

One step at a time.

Rinse and repeat.

Patience is hugely important…

Take a deep breath before you say another word. *Deeper breath.*

Go on a walk. Or a run. Or a car ride.

It's like the pissed-off email you don't send. Zip it, pops.

Also, praise your kids.

When they do something good, clap, cheer, go out for pizza at their favorite place. Not *your* favorite place, *their* favorite place.

But keep it real. Not everybody gets a trophy in life. For better or worse, the world doesn't work that way.

If your son or daughter has two left feet, they may not be destined to become a ballet dancer. At least not professionally. But they can still have a blast dancing around the house. Let them be themselves.

On the other hand, don't be afraid to tell the kids about things they're doing that could cause them harm and pain in the world lurking outside your house.

Do it gently.

Try not to be preachy.

(I know. I'm being a little preachy.)

Here's a little trick for giving advice to kids. Because *sometimes, they don't want to hear it from you.*

Maybe start by saying, "I'm sure you've already thought of this…" That usually gets them listening, gets them leaning in.

Another random thought: Clothes don't make the kid. It's not about what they're wearing, it's about who they are. *Inside.*

Teach them to be kind.

Kind kids don't make fun of other kids. Kind kids don't even make fun of their sibs. Not too much anyway.

~~~~~~~ 66 ~~~~~~~

"A lot of [parenting] is about the example you set for your kids—how you talk to them, how you talk to other people around them, and setting that example of what it means to be kind, polite, grateful, [and] honest."

—EMMY-, GRAMMY-, OSCAR-, AND TONY-WINNING ARTIST
JOHN LEGEND; TWO SONS, TWO DAUGHTERS

# Dealing with

# Screenagers

I f you were born in the Digital Dark Ages (before 1997), you have no idea what your kids are dealing with today.

The Internet was one thing. Social platforms are a whole different ball game. They're addictive. They're invasive. They're relentless. And they can be truly harmful to your kids' mental health.

Politicians and tech companies keep talking about making social sites safer for kids. But it's mostly just talk.

Meanwhile, these ubiquitous screens with their devious algorithms are taking over young people's lives.

Sorry. That got a little heavy.

So, what can a dad do? Make your kids use a landline?

No Freaking Way.

But you can lay down some laws. (Kindly and consistently, of course.)

No devices at the dinner table, for example. And that includes *your* phone.

Or no screen time when you're together in the car. (But they get to pick the playlist.)

There are even ways to set screen-time limits on your kids' devices. Don't ask me how. Just google it.

You can't monitor your child's social media use 24/7. And kids are very wily at finding work-arounds for restrictions. Even if you're pretty tech-savvy, trust me, the average middle schooler will leave you in the dust.

But if you start to see your kid preferring social media to human contact, or losing sleep because of screen time, take action.

It's dad time.

No,

We Didn't

Forget

About You.

How Could We?

## *You're Not a Dad…*
## *and That's 100 Percent Okay*

**W**hat about the guys who aren't dads?
Whether by choice or by circumstances, being a dad isn't for everyone.

Maybe you wanted children, but weren't in the right relationship at the right time.

Maybe you have a medical history that makes having kids challenging, or not possible.

Maybe you just…don't really want to spend all of your time with rug rats.

Perfectly understandable. For a while, I felt that way myself.

It's normal to question taking on a role so challenging, so draining—emotionally and financially—and so all-consuming.

But chances are, there are still plenty of "dad" opportunities for you.

You care about the world, its future, and the kids growing up in it.

Those kids may not be your own sons and daughters, but they need your help.

Everybody needs somebody who…

> …believes in them.
> …shows them how to get to where they're going.
> …makes them feel seen and heard.

My grandmother was that person for me. She taught me to work hard—with purpose—and to have a hell of a lot of fun doing it.

Her lesson was simple and to the point: "Hungry dogs run faster."

That doesn't mean they run alone.

Sign up. Pitch in. Show what you know. Show your stuff.

It's okay if you don't want to be a full-time dad. You have talent and experience to give.

Give to kids when they're young, and the gifts will last a lifetime:

Kids growing up and getting better jobs.

Kids developing a love for books.

Kids eventually being able to vote and figuring out who they want to vote for.

Kids living good lives.

### BE A MENTOR.

You work hard at your job. You've learned a lot about life. Don't keep it to yourself.

Recently, I was invited to speak at a conference on storytelling. The moderator was someone I knew years before. She told some stories about what I was like as a boss. I was touched to hear her use the word *inspiring*. What meant even more was when she pointed to one example I set—writing every day—as a key to her becoming a big-deal boss herself with a job she loves. *She* was inspiring that day.

## BE A COACH.

You played sports. You watch sports. You know sports.

Everyone remembers their favorite coach. The one who taught them how to throw a perfect football spiral, or a curve or slider in baseball.

The one who taught them how to lose a game without losing their cool.

Be that guy.

## BE AN UNCLE.

If you have a brother or sister with kids, you've got a potentially terrific role to play with your nieces and nephews. You know your brother or sister better than anyone. Their likes, their dislikes. What makes them laugh. What makes them cry. What makes them tick.

You can become just as close with their kids.

Spend time with those nieces and nephews. It doesn't matter whether it's planned or spontaneous.

Play catch.

Play Minecraft.

Find the last piece of a jigsaw puzzle—but let them put it in.

Come to school events.

Take pictures or home movies at graduation.

Cheer them on.

Never forget a birthday.

Take them on wild, mostly safe adventures.

Ask them for *their* opinion.

Tell them *yours.*

And one day when they have kids, you can be their favorite *great*-uncle.

Repeat

After Me:

"I'm a Good Guy,

I'm a Good Guy,

I'm a Good Guy..."

**S**ometimes, we just need to hear ourselves say it.

Deep down, most dads are sensitive. And vulnerable. And more than a little stubborn. Maybe we never entirely stop being little boys.

It's okay to talk about your feelings with the kids. It just might help you understand yourself a little better too.

The truth is, if you don't love and respect yourself, it's going to be hard to pass on love to your kids.

So look at yourself in the mirror every morning, first thing, and tell yourself you're okay. Every morning.

If it isn't morning right now, go to a mirror and tell yourself you're okay anyway.

You're a good guy, dad.

Just don't get carried away with yourself.

Here are some things worth thinking over:

Living healthier.

Whatever that means for your family.

Take walks together.

Take hikes together.

Climb mountains together.

Your kids are worth it.

You're worth it.

Walk away from abusing alcohol or drugs, and even cigarettes and vaping.

You might think that you can't do it, but you can do a whole lot better.

That's all we're talking about in this hour that we're spending together.

Doing better.

Not being perfect.

Just better.

# More
# Good Stuff

The rewards of being a better dad never stop, they just keep coming.

Kids with a strong attachment to their dads feel less anxious, less alone, less lost at sea.

We want that, right?

Well, we're in charge. At least partly in charge.

Think about your kids as much as you can. While you're shaving. When you're driving to work. During your lunch break. On your evening run. Or when you're just sitting in the old easy chair.

The rewards make every little, or big, sacrifice worth it. Ten times over.

Fathers can show daughters that they deserve respect from males. That's a huge thing you can do.

Good fathers have kids with higher self-esteem. That's a big one too.

They raise kids to be curious about the world.

They meet their kids' friends.

And if you do that, even some of that, chances are pretty good your kids will be your friends for life.

Our son now lives far away in big, bad New York City. But he calls a couple times a week.

I know Susan and I didn't do everything right. But we did a lot of little things okay.

And we can get better.

"My eight-year-old daughter,
out of the blue, announced one day that
she was definitely going to be an artist.
Some parents would say that's a crazy
idea. No! Let your kids run with it.
Our daughter has worked in museums all
over the world and ended up with a job
she loves at Christie's."

—JIM, CONSULTANT; THREE DAUGHTERS

# Better Dads

# Make Better

# Partners

**B**etter dads step up.

Better dads are full partners.

Better dads do their share of the dirty work.

Better dads give their partners a break once in a while.

Some dads told me they go to sleep holding hands with their partner. Sounds like a great, sane way to end the day.

Especially a tough day.

After all, you're in this together.

You're raising the precious babies you brought into the world.

Nothing can beat that. Nothing will ever be more important.

And that's a really good place to stop.

Our hour's up.

Let's have a beer. Or a soda. Or a cold lemonade.

You are now officially off the clock.

# Overtime

**W**ant to know more about how to be a better dad? These experts have been studying it for a lot longer than I have.

Here are some great books if you want to do a deeper dive.

~~~~~~~~~~~~~~~~~~~~~~~~~~~~~~~~~~~~~~~~~~~~~~~~~

*Presence: Bringing Your Boldest Self to Your Biggest Challenges* by Amy Cuddy

Manifest power and avoid the negative feedback loop: That's the strategic advice found in this book—based on social psychologist Amy Cuddy's famous TED Talk on "power poses"—about showing your best self to your entire family.

*There Are Dads Way Worse Than You: Unimpeachable Evidence of Your Excellence as a Father* by Glenn Boozan

This might look like a picture book, but it's definitely for grown-ups. If you're like me and into pop culture and history, you'll especially appreciate the references. Read this one when you've had a tough parenting day—you'll get a laugh and some reassurance.

*The New One: Painfully True Stories from a Reluctant Dad* by Mike Birbiglia, with poems by J. Hope Stein

In life and parenting, it helps to have a sense of humor. This comedian's take on becoming a dad shows the good, bad, and funny sides of parenthood.

~~~~~~~~~~~~~~~~~~~~~~~~~~~~~~~~~~~~~~~~~~~

*Things My Son Needs to Know About the World*
by Fredrik Backman

You might know Fredrik Backman from *A Man Called Ove* or *Anxious People.* This is something completely different, a series of lists and essays that show how fatherhood can be daunting, challenging, or rewarding—sometimes all three at once.

~~~~~~~~~~~~~~~~~~~~~~~~~~~~~~~~~~~~~~~~~~~

*Why Fathers Cry at Night: A Memoir in Love Poems, Letters, Recipes, and Remembrances* by Kwame Alexander

Kwame Alexander is a talented poet and author (together we wrote a book for kids, *Becoming Muhammad Ali*). He takes an emotional, introspective turn here to tell a story of love, especially his love for his daughters, through poems, letters, recipes, and essays.

# Let's Go to
# the Videotape

I f just two, or three, or five of these ideas work for you—you'll be a better dad, and that's one hour very well spent.

1. Be consistently fair. Trust really is built on consistency. And trust is everything.
2. Be a listener. Listen to your kids. Listen to your partner. Listen to yourself.
3. Learn how to say *I. Was. Wrong.* Just in case it ever happens.
4. Don't be afraid to say, "I love you." Say it now. Loud and proud.
5. Be a hugger. Hey, give yourself a hug every once in a while.
6. Tell your kids your story. Listen to theirs.
7. Read to your kids. Let them see books in your house.

8. Have your kids' backs. One day, they'll have yours.

9. Teach your kids to be responsible for their actions. And to be kind. That's the sweet spot—kindness.

10. Learn the value of the firm no.

11. Change the stinky diapers, get wet at bath time, sing the little darlings to sleep.

12. Be an all-world role model for your kids.

13. Don't argue in front of the kids.

14. Grow the fuck up. It's time.

15. Eat as a family. And eat healthy. Most of the time anyway.

16. Be a better dad and you'll be a better partner.

17. Find other dads to talk it out with.

It's been a real honor talking to you.

# Extra Credit

**B**efore I go, here's one more thought that might help.

Make a list of the things in your life that really piss you off.

The worst of the worst.

Stuff that makes your blood boil.

Makes you grit your teeth.

Now. Cross out everything you can't do anything about.

Just let it go.

Then maybe try to fix what's left on your list.

All the best to you. It's been an honor.

# ACKNOWLEDGMENTS

A lot of dads, and moms, and a few folks with no kids helped with this book. I want to single out just a few: Mark Ormson, Matt Eversmann, Dr. Brigid Balboni, Isabelle Morris, Bob Barnett, Ned Mahoney, Mike Lupica, Tim Malloy, John Keresty, Joe Denyeau, Bill Robinson, Ned Rust, Steve Bowen, Charles H. Patterson, Susan Solie Patterson.

## ABOUT THE AUTHOR

James Patterson is the most popular storyteller of our time. He is the creator of unforgettable characters and series, including Alex Cross, the Women's Murder Club, Jane Smith, and Maximum Ride, and of breathtaking true stories about the Kennedys, John Lennon, and Tiger Woods, as well as our military heroes, police officers, and ER nurses. Patterson has coauthored #1 bestselling novels with Bill Clinton, Dolly Parton, and Michael Crichton. He has told the story of his own life in *James Patterson by James Patterson* and received an Edgar Award, ten Emmy Awards, the Literarian Award from the National Book Foundation, and the National Humanities Medal.

# For a complete list of books by
# JAMES PATTERSON

## VISIT
## JamesPatterson.com

 Follow James Patterson on Facebook
**JamesPatterson**

 Follow James Patterson on X
**@JP_Books**

 Follow James Patterson on Instagram
**@jamespattersonbooks**

 Follow James Patterson on Substack
**jamespatterson.substack.com**

**Scan here to visit JamesPatterson.com
and learn about giveaways, sneak peeks,
new releases, and more.**

# Lucky in Love

## Jeanne Wagner Jordan

REVIEW AND HERALD PUBLISHING ASSOCIATION
Washington, DC 20039-0555
Hagerstown, MD 21740

Copyright © 1986 by
Review and Herald Publishing Association

This book was
Edited by Gerald Wheeler
Type set: 10/11 Bask.

PRINTED IN U.S.A.

**Library of Congress Cataloging in Publication Data**

Jordan, Jeanne Wagner, 1921-
  Lucky in love.

  1. Foster, Claudia. 2. Seventh-day Adventists—
United States—Biography. I. Title.
BX6193.F67J67    1987    286.7'32'0924    [B]    85-19417
ISBN 0-8280-0321-1

To my husband and my other three loves, my children

# —Prologue

The trouble with Army cots, Lucky thought, was that they were never long enough. Beds weren't either, for that matter. They were never built with anyone more than six feet in mind. Granted, it had been so long since he had slept in any kind of bed, his judgment on the point might be open to question. For the past few weeks, in fact, he hadn't even had a cot.

Foxes have holes, soldiers have foxholes, he mused. Sleeping on a cot was, in comparison, like resting on that cloud in the mattress ads back home. At first, at least, it had certainly felt like a cloud. Now after three days in the Fifth Army Hospital in Leghorn, Italy, his cot was becoming harder and shorter all the time.

But even worse than the thin mattress, he decided, were his grim surroundings. Lying there in the midst of a dozen or more field hospital beds holding the human wreckage of war was demoralizing enough—but knowing that he would soon be up on his feet and again in the front lines was scarcely a more cheering prospect.

He had been lucky this time, all right. The chart pinned on his government-issue, olive-drab blanket told just how lucky. He read it idly. "Sergeant Andrew Marshall, 3-618-595, Protestant, blood type O-negative, shrapnel fragment, right temple." Another fraction of an inch and that fragment would have missed his bone and penetrated his brain. A little to the right and it would have had his eye. Before he had ever had to dodge shrapnel and shells in Italy, his had been the kind of luck that had earned him his nickname "Lucky." The mortar explosion that knocked him flat and turned his Browning automatic rifle into a corkscrew had done him a favor, really. It knocked him, temporarily at least, right out of the heat of battle.

He remembered the devastating noise of it and waking up, disoriented, from a terrible dream, in which he was trying with his fingernails to dig a new hole of escape and there wasn't time! It couldn't have been very long, that dream. The medic he had seen before the blast giving plasma to his buddy down the slope was still holding the bottle aloft when he came to. His head hurt and blood ran down onto his pants from somewhere. Putting his hand to his cheek, he found it warm and wet. Then he crawled down the hill to the medic.

"Sorry, pal, got my hands full," the medic told him. "You look as if you can make it on your own to the aid station. It's only about a kilometer. *Keep low,* though."

The medic had been right. He did have his hands full. Too many others, unable to move, were awaiting his attention, friends he had known all these months. Some were too far gone to need a medic; he could see that as he crawled and crouched from tree to tree. What was it the medic had said? *Keep low.* No problem! He did not feel the least temptation to "stand up tall," as his mother had always told him when he was a kid. In the din of artillery fire and the flash of explosion, he kept wishing, for the first time since he passed the six-foot marker on the wall at home, that he were shorter. One thing was sure. Not every kilometer measured the approximate half mile he had learned in high school physics. The one to the aid station was at least three miles long!

Once or twice he thought he was going to pass out, whether from pain or fear, he couldn't tell. Sweat trickling down his back, blood streaming into his eyes and mouth, he had hardly felt prepared for what happened next. Into the bloody blur of his vision suddenly loomed three enemy soldiers. Flushed out of hiding by some turn of events— perhaps a direct hit on their hideout—they had run right into his path. In a reflex action faster than he thought himself capable of, he barked out a command in German to halt, brandished his only weapon, a hand grenade, and ordered them to precede him, hands up.

As he lay in the hospital tent thinking back on the ironical twist—a minor act of heroism forced on a wounded infantryman—Lucky could not help grinning. What must the fellows at the aid station have thought as a bloodstained GI turned over his captives to them and then crumpled into a muddy heap at their feet.

Events after that were something of a blur in his mind. The medics had finally put him onto a truck that took him to Leghorn with a load of GIs a lot less lucky than he. Put to sleep with sodium pentothal, the fragment removed, he had awakened later with a monumental pain throbbing in his head. A nurse was jabbing him with a long needle—full of a new miracle drug he'd heard someone call penicillin—and reciting to him the inevitable line, "You're lucky, soldier." She said he'd be out of there in a week or less.

Lucky calculated quickly. He had been wounded on the fourteenth. Today was what? He had lost track. His eyes traveled over the bandaged bodies around him and found the calendar on the bare gray wall at the end of the room. April 17, 1945. *April 17!* That was a date he couldn't forget, try as he would. Five years ago, April 17, 1940, was the day he had met Claudia. In fact, he had seen her picture the year before that, and it was with the picture he had first fallen in love.

Turning over on his side, he found his parka rolled up on the floor by his cot. Digging into a deep pocket, he pulled out his billfold and strung open the foldout containing his pictures: Mom, Dad, sis, a couple of girls from here and there, and—Claudia. It was the wallet-sized photo she had given him after they met. Ragged at the corners and battle-scarred by now, it was in worse shape, no doubt, than the 8 x 10 original he had seen that April day back in 1939 . . .

\* \* \*

Spring was in the air as Lucky Marshall jumped out of Mr. Bailey's truck (Bailey's Market, Fresh Fruit, Vegetables, and Meat, Come in Today) and walked to the back door of the neat frame house, two bags of groceries in his arms. Whistling as usual, he bounded up the steps, taking care to avoid a mateless roller skate standing dangerous guard at the door. That would be Jennifer's, he thought. Chocolate fingerprints stood out in bold relief on the kitchen door, betraying a premature raid on the Easter basket. Those would be little Eric's. With a smile Lucky recalled his own crimes against cookie jars and bread boxes in his hungry young years.

Leaning one bag against his knee, he rapped out a shave-and-a-haircut knock. While he waited, he drank in the sweet Saturday morning fragrance. The long Northern winter was finally over, and he felt as carefree and buoyant as the cardinal serenading him from a branch overhead. At the moment he couldn't think of a single problem, unless maybe he should be wondering if he could win the half mile at the state track meet coming up. Winning at track and football had become a way of life these past years and lent a certain authenticity to his nickname. Yes, he was lucky all right and glad to be alive.

Mrs. Preston came to the door. She was a regular customer of Bailey's and a special friend of his. Admittedly, it was a friendship he himself had cultivated as he made his rounds delivering grocery orders. He greatly admired her as a homemaker—the kind he would want for a wife when he could think of marrying: intelligent, pretty, friendly, and a good cook. From experience he knew about her cooking. By carefully timing his stops, he had mastered the moment to arrive at her door just when she was finishing off her weekly baking. She never failed to offer him a sample roll or cookie or piece of pie.

"Hello, Lucky," she said. "I was hoping you'd get here soon. I need the eggs for Jennifer's birthday cake. I want to make it this morning while she and Eric are at their cousins'. I don't suppose you have time for a cinnamon roll and a glass of milk?"

"I don't suppose you remember who you are talking to, madam," Lucky joked. "The name is Marshall, and I have a blanket permission from Mr. Bailey to take whatever time is necessary to eat one of Mrs. Preston's cinnamon rolls."

"Then why did he have to call you up to remind you to check back in at the store last Saturday?" the woman teased.

"Who would ever have thought it would take me a half hour to eat three cookies and report my exploits in the semifinals at Newburg! But Mr. Bailey's an understanding man," he assured her. "And," he added, "a discerning one. He knows the best cooks on the route. That's why he called here first to find me!"

"Well, come on in the dining room with your snack. This room's like an oven. Besides, I need a breather before I start the cake." Mrs. Preston led him from the kitchen into the cheerful dining room. "You haven't told me how the last weeks of school are going. Did you get your sports copy ready for the annual on time? When's the big track meet? Do you know who your graduation speaker will be?"

"There's a half hour's worth of questions right there," Lucky said, installing himself at the table and beginning his treat. Between leisurely swallows, he answered the battery of questions she had asked. Then as he rose to take his empty glass to the kitchen, his eyes fell on a sparkling new picture frame sitting on the buffet near the door, containing a portrait he hadn't seen before.

"Hey," he said, whistling softly, "this is nice, and I'm not talking about the frame! Who is she, Mrs. Preston?"

"That's my sister Claudia. Remember? I told you I had a sister graduating from high school this year, too. Back in my hometown."

"Sa-ay, she certainly looks like you. Same brown eyes, same smile."

"People tell me that," Gladys Preston replied, obviously pleased.

"I'd like to meet her," Lucky remarked on his way to the door. "Let me know if she's ever in town. Thanks for the rolls," he said over his shoulder as he took the back steps in a single stride. "See you next week."

"Good luck at the track meet, Lucky," she called after him.

Lucky placed second in the state track meet, as it turned out, but it was a year before he met Claudia. High school was over, but college was no option at all. He had no funds for that. But he did have a job at the local furnace factory, and his standing with the young social set in town was solid. With some new clothes, a growing savings account, and enough leisure time for sports, dances, and other amusements, he was leading a secure small-town life that seemed destined to go on indefinitely.

Then one April day, heading for the park for his first tennis set of the season, he passed the Preston home, only a block from the courts. Realizing he was ahead of his partner by a few minutes, he retraced his steps on impulse and turned in at the gate. No longer a Saturday delivery boy, he had had little excuse to visit with Mrs. Preston the past year. It was just possible the current grocery boy hadn't taken the last cookie in the jar.

At the door he greeted young Eric heartily and shook his hand. "Hello there, fella, remember me?"

The boy grinned and invited him in. At the same moment, 6-year-old Jennifer sidled shyly out of the living room, coloring book and crayon still in hand. As she flashed him a wide smile with two missing front teeth, he noted an air of expectancy about her that told him something special was afoot.

"You know what?" she started to say, ushering him into the living room. But she didn't need to finish. With one glance, Lucky *knew* what. On the floor amidst scattered pieces of a jigsaw puzzle sat a girl of, he quickly judged, about 19.

"Hello, you must be Claudia," he said, feeling a little awkward and wishing someone would make a proper introduction.

"Yes, how did you know?" she asked, surprised.

"No one could resemble Mrs. Preston so much without being her sister. And besides, you also look a little like your picture."

"A very clever deduction," Claudia said in mock Sherlock Holmes tones. "But I can top that. I've never seen your picture, but something"—she gave a knowing look in the direction of Eric—"tells me you are Lucky Marshall."

That was the way it all started. Claudia had come for only a short visit that lengthened in proportion to her increasing interest in Lakeville, more particularly in one of its native sons. In due time, the recommendation of a cousin and the influence of George Preston helped her find a job in an office in town, and she settled down for an indefinite stay. Lucky's visits to the Preston home became even more regular than when he used to deliver groceries there on Saturdays.

Both Gladys and George approved of the young couple "going steady." They seemed right for each other. Claudia, slender and vivacious, made up in warmth and wit what she lacked in real beauty, but she was pretty enough, and Lucky thought her just right in every way. She could always counter with exactly the right thrust when he teased; she had just the sense of humor he appreciated. She was Gladys' sister all right, but she was—though he would certainly never let Mrs. Preston know—much more the ideal woman than the latter had once personified.

Lucky felt only one reservation, in fact, about Claudia. She never went to church. Not any church at all. Because he was not very serious about religion himself, he could quite easily ignore his misgivings about her lack of church affiliation, but he did regularly invite her to attend services with him.

"Come with me tomorrow," he suggested one Saturday night as they walked home from the movies. "It would please my mom so much."

"I'm sorry, Lucky. I like your mother very much, and I'd do anything to please her—anything, except go to church. It's just not natural for me. I'd feel like a fish out of water."

"Where did you ever get such an aversion to church?"

"I don't know if it's an aversion or not. I've never once been to church, you know. So I can't say if it's church itself or the *idea* of it that bothers me. It's something my dad ingrained in me from as long as I can remember. To him the church is the scarlet woman of the Apocalypse, the real antichrist or something."

"But if your dad isn't a Christian, how does he know about the Apocalypse and all that?"

"Oh, but he is a Christian, definitely," Claudia quickly replied. "In fact, he comes from a strong Lutheran background. But somewhere in his early married years, long before I was born, he dropped out, disillusioned about something, I've never known what. For a while he took up with the writings of a Pastor Russell, I think his name was."

"You mean the *Jehovah's Witnesses?*" Lucky exclaimed with disrelish. Although he admired the zeal and sincerity of their members, small sects had always put him off because he felt that they brought reproach on the name of Christianity.

"No, as soon as the Russellites became Witnesses, Papa withdrew from them, and ever since he's opposed organized churches more and more. It's become a real passion with him. And it's rubbed off on me, too. I can't overcome my upbringing, that's all."

Lucky was silent. His own background was the exact opposite. Ever since he could remember, his parents had taken him to Sunday school and church. They were pillars in their church, and the church itself was highly respected in Lakeville. Why his parents had chosen this one denomination over others in the community, he did not know. It was nearby, it was Protestant, it did not represent a sect. That apparently was enough.

"I think if you went just once, Claudia," he began, but she broke in.

"Lucky, look at the time! Do you think I could ever get up before ten tomorrow morning to go to church? Just tell your mom it's your fault for keeping me up so late on Saturday

PROLOGUE

nights."

That was as far as they got on the subject of churchgoing,
and they never otherwise mentioned religion. They had
other more urgent matters to discuss, marriage for one.
They agreed that they were still too young to think of getting
married. But think of it they did, as Lucky continued to save
more money, and Claudia followed the prevailing tradition
for brides-to-be and began a hope chest. They might have
married in a year or two if an abrupt turn of events at
Founders Furnace hadn't changed everything.

One day Lucky arrived at the shop to find most of the
men already there, some milling around outside the payroll
window, others standing in knots of two or three talking in
low tones. He looked for his time card. It wasn't in its slot.
None of the slots contained cards.

"What's up?" he asked a man nearby.

"Looks as if there's a shutdown at Founders Furnace for
a while. Six months at least, they say—while they go through
the books."

"But without any warning?"

"Right. Seems something big happened up front. Not so
bad for you, Lucky. You're single."

"Yeah, I know how tough it'll be for you, Rudy, with your
family and all. Sure hope you can find something else right
away."

"If I were single," the other continued, "you know what
I'd do? I'd drive my uncle Howard to Florida for the winter.
He's been looking for someone. Since his heart attack he's
not able to drive, and yet he needs to get there, the doctor
says."

Only half listening, Lucky was still trying to grasp the
idea of being laid off. He could see himself now, *un*lucky
Lucky, hanging around town with no visible means of
support.

"Why don't *you* offer to do it, man? Howard says it's easy
to get a job in a restaurant or hotel during the winter
months. And think of the fun you could have in the
sun—while we shovel snow up here. I'll tell my uncle to get

15

in touch with you, all right, Lucky?"

"H'm? Yeah, sure," Lucky murmured, all the while thinking what his next move should be and not quite certain just what Rudy had been talking about. "Sure thing, Rudy."

They hung around for a while, these suddenly jobless men, who had only just gotten accustomed to steady work after the long years of the depression. But most did not linger long. If other jobs were available, it was no good wasting time talking. The yard soon emptied, and Lucky joined the others pouring out the gate to begin their frantic search for work. Although he went from one prospect to the next until late afternoon, luck seemed against him this time. He found nothing.

His normally high spirits dampened, he made his way to the Prestons' house that evening to see Claudia, whom he had hoped to be able to tell of another job just found. She could, in any case, be counted on to cheer him up. He found her washing dishes and automatically picked up the dish towel to dry.

"I heard the bad news at the office today, Lucky," Claudia said, broaching the subject he was reluctant to mention. He nodded his head.

The telephone rang in the hall, and Eric came thumping down the stairs, two at a time, calling, "I think it's for me. I'll get it."

A minute later he poked his head into the kitchen. "For you, Lucky. Boy, they sure know where to find you, all right!"

Lucky went to the phone. Over the splash of water and clatter of dishes, Claudia heard little of the conversation, except at the end. "Sure, Howard, I'll think it over and let you know right away."

When he returned to the kitchen, he seemed puzzled and preoccupied. "That was Howard James," he reported. "Wants to know if I'd be interested in driving him to Florida and staying the winter. He has friends in St. Petersburg who will help me find a job. Can you beat that? Why me?"

"Why you? Because he knows you're a steady, non-drinking fellow out of a job, and a good driver, that's why.

What did you tell him? You'll do it, of course?"

"And leave you? Not on your life!"

"Why not? Just think, a paid trip to Florida, and a whole winter away from the snow and cold. I'd do it, if I were you. Especially now, with your job gone."

"Claudia, do you realize what you're saying so casually? That's six months of separation. Why, who knows, someone else might come along and take my place. Bad enough to lose my job—I don't want to lose my girl besides!"

He was half joking, she knew, and Claudia acted dutifully shocked at the suggestion. "If that's the only thing that's holding you back," she said, drying her hands and putting her arms around his neck, "then hurry over to that telephone and tell Mr. James you're packed and ready to go. Nobody else is going to take your place, you know that."

"I think you're actually trying to get rid of me," he commented, trying by teasing to change the subject.

"No, I'm not. I'd miss you very much," she responded, suddenly quite serious. "I know you wonder why I'm encouraging you to go, Lucky. For one thing, I'd never forgive myself if I kept you from a trip like this. Why, it's a *wonderful* chance for you."

"And for another?"

"Well, for another thing, I . . . I think it might be good for us. I've been thinking a lot lately about the future and wondering if we should be talking about marriage until we're really sure of ourselves. Separation might help us find out how much we actually care for each other. Anyway, what's that saying about absence making the heart grow fonder?"

"There's no way mine can grow fonder of you, honey. No, ma'am, I'm not going to leave you just to find out something I already know."

"Go to Florida, Lucky. I insist. You'll never be sorry. And I'll be waiting for you when you come back, I promise."

And that was how he, Lucky Marshall, had found himself in Florida that winter of '40. True to her promise, his girl, Claudia Foster, *was* waiting for him six months later when he returned. But it was a different Claudia, and he realized she would never be the same again . . .

"Who's that, pal, your girl?"

The muffled voice emanating from the bandages in the next cot brought Lucky suddenly back to the reality of Leghorn, Italy. He was still holding Claudia's picture. Even after four years of separation, seeing her face stirred his pulse. Other girls had come and gone, but none that ever quite matched her. He wondered what she was doing now on April 17, *their* day.

"No," he answered as he folded up his wallet and put it back into his parka pocket, "it's just someone . . . I used to know . . . back home."

\* \* \*

Claudia sat down at the desk in her room in the dorm and opened her notebook. Determined to get her book review done that morning, she uncapped her fountain pen and began to write the date. April . . . April what? The calendar she looked at was spangled with the wartime "Keep 'Em Flying" legend in bold red, white, and blue stars. It was only one of the evidences in the room of the disturbing conflict raging far away. A photograph of the soldier her roommate would be marrying someday when he came back from the South Seas—*if* he came back; another picture of her own Navy-uniformed brother; V-mail letters scattered on the bed and in neat stacks on both desks—they were ever-present reminders of a war the dorm girls, on their peaceful campus, found hard to believe real. Their minds preoccupied most of the time with assignments and work, they were able to keep at bay the anxiety and fears they all felt for the writers of those V-mail messages at the various far-flung fronts in Europe, North Africa, and the South Pacific.

With firm, down-to-business strokes, Claudia wrote the date on her paper: April 17, 1945. The very day, five years ago, she realized with a start, that she had met Lucky Marshall! Putting down the pen, she stared at the paper in front of her. No use now to try to concentrate on her review. She reached into a drawer and pulled out a note that had come from Gladys that morning, along with a clipping from the Lakeville *Daily*. So Lucky had been wounded. He was in a hospital, the article said, "somewhere in Italy." She wondered how badly he was hurt, if he was in pain, if he had been disfigured or dismembered in any way.

"Dear Lord," she breathed, "don't let anything like that have happened, not to *Lucky.*" Again she read the short clipping. Not a thing there to relieve a person's mind. Just that his parents had received a wounded-in-action telegram, the routine notice from the government, coming far too often to homes across the nation. Probably even they had no more information than that.

She thought about sending him a letter. All the girls wrote to two or three servicemen, no matter how casual the acquaintance. It was your patriotic duty. Still, the last time she saw him, he hadn't asked her to write. What a shock when he walked into the office that day while she was at work—already nearly a year ago now. She couldn't have been more taken aback to see General Eisenhower himself standing across the counter saying, "Hello, Claudia."

Just as if it had been the day before instead of three years since Lucky had last said those words. How handsome he looked in his uniform! On furlough before shipping out, he had learned from Gladys, he told her, where she worked at the college and her hours. Then he had driven the twenty miles from Lakeville just to tell her he was going overseas, going into combat, he didn't know where. And to ask for her prayers.

How quick, in her confusion, she had been to promise them, and in a voice she could hardly raise above a whisper, to wish him her best. Hoping he couldn't see the pulse thumping wildly in her throat and the flush she felt burning her cheeks, she waited for his next words.

"Goodbye, Claudia," he said. That was all. Not a word about writing, or hoping to see her again when he got back—*if* he got back.

She did pray for him after that, more so at first than lately. Prayers had become routine bless-everyone words, quickly poured out as she sank into bed at night exhausted. A heavy classload as her graduation from college drew nearer and the long hours at the office involved in working one's way were crowding out almost any other concern. Besides, by concerted effort to forget him, she had allowed Lucky to become quite remote, almost unreal. She had given up all hopes for them that night back in River Bend when she had handed him his ring . . .

* * *

"Why am I so *nervous?*" The question was a rhetorical one, posed mostly to the mirror, as Claudia combed her hair for the third or fourth time in the last half hour. Any moment now Lucky would be ringing the bell, and it would be like old times. Certainly nothing to be nervous about. But would things be the same between them? So much had happened in her own life the past months to change her. Maybe Lucky had changed too.

Minutes later when she opened the door to him, she knew he hadn't—in appearance, anyway. Still tall, curly-haired, handsome, he hugged her to him, though with the restraint called for by the presence of another in the room.

"Come in, Lucky," Claudia said, more breathless from the nervousness she was still feeling than the warmth of the greeting. "There's more of my family to meet—Helen, this is Lucky Marshall."

"As if I didn't know already who was coming," Helen laughed. "I'm another sister of Claudia's, you know. We've been so pleased to have her with us these past few months since she lost her job in Lakeville."

"I'm glad to meet the Mrs. Johnson I've been writing 'in-care-of' so often these days. Thanks for taking Claudia in. I guess when the factory in Lakeville closed last year, a lot of other jobs ran out. It's really great she has sisters like you and Gladys."

"Please sit down. I'll call the other half of the 'in-care-of.' He's in the garage tinkering. I think he was trying to lure me there, too. Something about the young people wanting to be alone. I'm afraid I didn't cooperate—I was too curious to see

Claudia's famous Lucky!"

"A family trait, curiosity." Lucky remembered Claudia's efforts to get him to let her open ahead of time the Christmas and birthday presents he had for her. They exchanged knowing smiles.

"It most certainly does run in the family." The voice came from the kitchen. Then Mark Johnson entered the room drying his hands, and extended his right one to Lucky. "Glad to meet you at last. Sit down, please."

Lucky took Claudia's hand and pulled her down beside him on the sofa, and the four were soon chatting comfortably. Claudia's heartbeat had slowed almost to normal, her nervousness fast disappearing.

"We can see you've been to Florida, all right," Mark commented. "After our hard winter here Claudia looks as pale as a sheet next to your tan."

"She looks great to me." Lucky squeezed the small white hand in his brown one.

"Now that my curiosity is satisfied," Helen said, "I must excuse myself and start supper. You'll join us, of course, Lucky."

"That's a tempting invitation, Mrs. Johnson. If good cooking, like curiosity, runs in your family, as it seems to, you can probably match even Gladys' high quality. But I was hoping to take Claudia to the new Chinese restaurant on Route 50 I've heard so much about since I got back."

"Oh, I'd love that. I haven't had Chinese food for ages." Claudia's compliance gave him to understand that she was as eager to be alone with him as he was with her. She wondered how he would feel if he knew why.

Across the table from him at the Golden Dragon, her nervousness returned as she began, "I could hardly wait to see you, Lucky. I have the most wonderful surprise for you. It was even too big to write you about. I've been saving it all this time."

"I'm all ears, honey."

Claudia hesitated, studying the menu absently. "I don't quite know how to tell you."

"Well, you're awfully serious about something that's supposed to be a surprise. I know! *You're* going off to Florida next winter," he joked.

Her smile faded almost at once. "Do you remember before you left for the South how you were always inviting me to church with you on Sunday?"

"How could I forget! You know how much it worried me that someday I was going to marry a regular little heathen."

His banter provided just the cue she needed. "Well, I'm not a 'little heathen' any longer," she announced. "I'm a Seventh-day Adventist."

"Wait just a minute, Claudia! You didn't *mean* that! Make it Methodist or Baptist or even Catholic—as strange as that may sound, coming from a staunch Protestant. But don't tell me you've joined one of those *cults!*"

"It's not a cult, Lucky, honest. Let me tell you what Seventh-day Adventist means."

"You don't have to tell me. I know. It means no more dances, no more movies, no more fun. It means going to a storefront church—and on *Saturday* at that."

Taken aback by the vehemence of his reaction, she sat silently for a stunned moment. The waiter came, and Lucky gave their order. He took no apparent notice that Claudia preferred the vegetable chow mein to his sweet-sour pork. When the waiter had left, she broached the matter again, determined to put her position in the proper perspective. As she talked, her enthusiasm mounted, and before the meal ended she had delved not only into the seventh-day question but various Old and New Testament prophecies, along with what really would happen during the millennium, and why it was better to be a vegetarian.

The deeper she went, the more she knew she was spoiling the whole surprise. But as she leapfrogged from Genesis to Revelation, she could not restrain her eagerness to prove she did not belong to a cult and that she had found truth. She had been so sure she would need only tell him how reasonable it all was to convince him that she had.

"Well, you've certainly thrown the book at me, Claudia.

Let's get out of here. I've had enough religion for one night!"

Obviously distraught, Lucky called for the check, propelled her from the restaurant, and drove her home. In the car, no further word passed between them on this or any other subject. Tears stung her eyes as she pondered the letdown of his reaction. Her first witness for God, and she had ruined it.

At the door Lucky drew her to him. "Don't worry, darling. You'll get over this. You're just carried away right now. It's only a passing fancy. You'll get over it, you'll see."

Claudia pushed him gently away. "No, Lucky, I'll never get over it. I'm committed to being an Adventist. It's the most important thing that's ever happened to me."

"More important even than . . . me?"

"Yes."

"If you had to make a choice?"

There was a long pause as the impact of what he had said sank in.

"I've made my choice already, Lucky." She slipped off her ring, thrust it in his hand, and fled into the house.

\* \* \*

Claudia put the clipping back in the desk drawer and picked up her pen again. Still lost in thought, she looked out across a campus just coming to life at the end of the harsh winter. Jonquils bloomed yellow against the emerald expanse of lawn. It had been just such a day when she met Lucky. They were so young then, full of dreams that ended abruptly only a year later. Helen told her afterward that perhaps she needn't have broken off at Lucky's first reaction to her new commitment. But he had never even called her after that, never asked her to change her mind. What if he had not gone to Florida in the first place? What if, what if?

As she shook herself from her reverie she had not the least doubt that all things had worked together for good, that it was in God's providence, the way it all happened.

# PART II

# In Retrospect: The
# Way It All Happened

Claudia heard the doorbell ring downstairs as she was folding the last blouse to put in her suitcase. No need for her to go down and answer. It wouldn't be for her, anyway, with Lucky in Florida for the winter. Probably some salesman or one of those door-to-door people handing out religious tracts. She continued her packing.

"Come on down, Claudia," Gladys called. "Helen's here and Mark, too."

Their sister Helen. How long had it been since they'd seen her? Months, maybe a year. And she lived only twenty-five miles away. Claudia tried to shut the suitcase, but the lid would not go down. She'd have to unload some things or sit on it. Later, after the visitors left, she'd work on it. Now she must get downstairs and greet them. Funny how you could feel like a stranger with your own sister.

"Hi, Helen. Hi, Mark. What brings you to the thriving metropolis of Lakeville?"

"The big-city lights, my dear. Like moths to a candle, we're lured here every so often." Mark was always joking about small-town Lakeville. As if River Bend were a Chicago or New York! She had hit on a good opener, all right.

The three sisters and two brothers-in-law soon engaged in shop and weather talk, almost, Claudia thought, as if they were skirting a heavier subject she felt sure was bound to arise in the conversation—the Johnsons' new religion. It was the reason the rest of their large family steered rather clear of them, though come to think of it, they themselves had never raised the matter first. It was usually their father who got into it with them, and the scene nearly always turned turbulent in the end. Dad always got so "het up"! People ought to avoid talking about politics and religion, she thought. Neither one was safe to discuss.

"And what are you up to these days?" she heard Helen asking.

"Who, me?" Claudia realized she had drifted out of the conversation. "As a matter of fact, right now I'm packing to go back home to Chesterfield. Back to 'the ranch.' My job just ran out."

"Well, you'll be stuck on the ranch, you know. There's nothing going on there, especially in winter when the resort crowd is gone. Better come on over to River Bend and look around first. You're welcome to stay with us."

"Thanks, Mark." She searched her mind for an excuse. Staying with the Johnsons was the last thing she wanted to do, though ever since graduation—until she got her job in Lakeville—Helen had been writing her to come. But she had never even gone for a visit. Although she didn't know much about their religion, what she had heard was enough to keep her away. All those fanatical ideas about the seven last plagues and the end of the world. At not quite 20 she was too young to worry about the world coming to an end.

No, she could not possibly accept. But her mind was totally blank. Not one plausible reason for not going to River Bend with her sister and brother-in-law occurred to her. Except, of course, for that stubborn lid, she was already packed. She hadn't bought her bus ticket yet. And she hadn't even called home to let the folks know. If only she had done at least one of these things, she would have something to offer as a reason.

"I—I guess I could try that," she heard herself saying. Then she felt like biting her tongue. What had she gotten herself into! Just because she didn't have the nerve to say No—that she didn't *want* to stay with them—she was stuck. Well, she would go. But one thing was sure, she would not let them pressure her into attending their church. They weren't going to change her into a religious recluse!

After successively declining George Preston's offer of cigarettes, beer, and coffee, the Johnsons agreed to stay for supper—where they turned down the proffered cold cuts, sliced ham, and apple pie. Why the pie? Claudia wondered. What was wrong with flour and lard, anyway? As things became more awkward, even Mark's heroic efforts to make a joke of their odd eating habits failed. Claudia was more sure than ever she had let herself in for a dull few days ahead. And it was going to be only a few days, she promised herself. If she found a job, she would look for a place to stay—YWCA, maybe. And if she didn't find work in a few days, well, Chesterfield, local girl comes home!

"We really must be on our way," Helen said, helping her sisters clear the table. At the same time she was thinking ahead as to where they would put Claudia's things in their small house, and how they would handle a number of problems bound to arise. Maybe Mark should not have invited her into their cloistered home. But it was too late now, and no use to worry. The Lord would help them handle everything.

They loaded Claudia's suitcases and bits and pieces into the trunk of their car and soon headed down the highway. After a few miles, Claudia relaxed and comforted herself with the thought that one thing in favor of River Bend over Chesterfield was that it was closer to Lakeville, when Lucky came back. Mark quizzed her about her former job, teased her about Lucky, and warned her that in remote River Bend mail from Florida got delivered only once a month, if that often. Claudia found herself laughing and protesting as if unaware of the dismal existence she expected to have to endure.

\* \* \*

"So this is where you live," she said as she entered the Johnsons' living room.

"Yes, unless I got lost and we are actually in the city zoo," Mark teased. "Or did you expect something different about our place?"

"No, that is, I . . ."

Helen came to her rescue. "I know. You expected something unusual—an offering box at the entrance, votive candles burning, or incense—something to announce that religious fanatics live here!"

"Yes," Claudia replied, relieved to have her feelings understood and defused by Helen's exaggeration. "I mean No. I didn't think of anything as exotic as that, but . . . well, you know, Helen and Mark, we all—the whole family—feel you've turned rather—uh—eccentric. I guess I expected austerity, maybe, or even poverty, because Dad says you give about everything you earn to your church."

Helen laughed indulgently. "I wish we gave as much as they think we do. We'd love to bestow all our goods to feed the poor and give our bodies to be burned if that would help. But the best we can do is 'charity'—which is a pun you may not understand until you read 1 Corinthians 13. Anyway," she added quickly, to divert the trend away from religious overtones, "we've grown used to being ostracized by the family. Do you know you're the first one to visit us in three years?"

"That's terrible, Helen. It really is," her sister said lamely, wondering what the pun was all about. She loved puns herself and would try to sneak a look in the Bible and figure it out. If she could find where Corinthians was.

"But what makes me feel so bad now that you're here is that I'm gone a lot in the evenings, giving Bible lessons. And on Friday nights I have to be at young people's meeting because I'm the leader."

A startling fact registered in Claudia's mind. *Her sister's church had young people in it!* But *how* young? Helen's age? She wasn't so young—why, she was in her 30s already! Could there be any members younger than that? The whole thing piqued her curiosity—that old family trait again. This time she'd stave it off and not pursue the matter.

For her part, Helen was trying to hold in check all her impulses. That was *all* she was going to say about her church—for the moment.

"Don't worry about me, Helen. I'll find something to do

while you're gone."

* * *

Claudia sat among the job applicants at Fidelity Bank and Trust, waiting nervously to be called for an interview. As the door to the inner office closed behind the next in line, her tension mounted. It was the first place that had granted her an interview. Three days of filling out forms and being told "we'll call you if we need you" had led to this moment.

Did she dare dream a job awaited her behind the oak panels she was hopefully staring at? Working in a bank, what *prestige!* She envisioned herself dressed in a smart but conservative suit, walking purposely through the corridors and among the desks of this handsome suite, exchanging words with this secretary and that supervisor, handing an impeccably typed report to Mr. Big himself. Ideal working conditions and pleasant surroundings seemed to be the order of the day here. The busy hum of voices and machines, muffled in carpet and acoustical ceiling, soothed her jitters as she waited.

"Miss Foster?"

It was her turn! She picked up her purse and followed the secretary to the office of Mr. William J. Berry (so the plaque on the door told her) on the other side of the oak panels. "This is Claudia Foster, Mr. Berry."

He gestured for her to sit down as he studied her application. Now the stage fright struck again as she waited. She wished her shoes were shinier and her nose less shiny. Somehow her plush chair made her "little basic black dress" seem a bit shabby.

"Miss Foster, we have an opening in our billing department that we think—with your experience in Lake-ville—you may be qualified for. Your application and references are in order." He paused as his eyes ran down the form. "Except here—I see you left a blank where we've asked for your religious affiliation."

"It's because I have none."

The man looked up quickly. "Well, I realize a person's religious persuasion—or lack of it—has little to do with her job qualifications. Actually, we only include that question in order to be aware of any special circumstances our employees' needs may demand. Your folks at home have no church group either?"

The interview was taking a strange twist. Why was he interested in this area of her life? "Not really. But then I don't live at home."

"This address you give is not your home address then?"

"Well, no. I'm staying with my sister and brother-in-law for the time being."

"They don't go to any church?"

Claudia bit her lip. Why had she brought up Mark and Helen? Surely where she lived was none of his concern, much less the habits of her family members. Now he had probed into their private lives.

"Yes, they go to the Seventh-day Adventist Church," she said when the silence stretched uncomfortably, and wished she hadn't said anything, that she were back in Lakeville or Chesterfield, or just anywhere else.

"Adventists, are they? You know, Miss Foster, we work in this office on Saturday morning."

"I understand, Mr. Berry. I have no problem with that."

The bank official studied her a long minute. "Well, all right. I didn't mean to dwell on this matter. I was only curious about your leaving that space blank, and I got going from there. Myself, I'm Catholic." He swiveled around and glanced out the window, then continued, his back still half turned to her. "If you're sure no unusual habits of yours"—here he faced her directly—"will interfere with your work, you have the job."

"Thank you, sir," Claudia said, hoping the words showed just the right balance of appreciation and restraint. "When do I begin?"

"Monday morning at eight-thirty. Report to Mrs. Sanders."

After closing the door softly behind her, Claudia allowed herself the grin of relief and satisfaction she had carefully suppressed until she left Mr. Berry's office, and hurried—

almost ran—out into the cold January air, glowingly warm inside.

On the bus home she listened to the tires singing to the seams in the pavement, "I've got a job, I've got a job." The brakes squealed it at every stop; the change in the coin box jingled the same tune.

Racing up the steps to the Johnsons' house, she called, "Helen, guess what? I got a job in the billing department at Fidelity Bank! Helen, are you here?"

"Doing the laundry. Come on down." Her sister's voice came from the basement. "Never mind. I'll be right up. I need to make some starch."

Excited and happy, Claudia reported all the details of her interview, except the part she still felt so strange and uncalled for, the allusion to Helen and Mark's religion.

"Well, good. Now that's settled, and you'll be on the receiving end of a paycheck again. I suppose . . . you'll work five days a week, Monday through Friday, no doubt?"

"No, actually we work Saturday mornings at Fidelity, Mr. Berry says. But that's not bad. I'll still have all Saturday afternoon to do my washing and ironing and shopping."

"Let's go have some lunch while I'm upstairs." Helen quickly changed the subject, but Claudia's excitement over the success of her venture kept her from noticing the disappointment in her sister's eyes at the news about Saturday.

So, Helen thought, she was to work all Saturday morning. Why, that way she would never be able to visit church. And wash and iron here in their house on Sabbath? In what strange way had the Lord answered her private morning prayer that He would find just the right job for her sister? "Somehow, Lord," she breathed, as they went into the kitchen, "You work it out."

\* \* \*

Claudia spent a long weekend from Thursday on in Chesterfield, visiting her parents. She wanted to explain her move to River Bend and report in person the good news about her job. Early Sunday afternoon she returned to her new home with the Johnsons, her father's half-jocular warning about not letting them make an "Advent" of her still fresh in her mind.

The first week of work was a hard one, of course. Claudia was more than glad when the clock on the wall in her department ticked off the closing time each day. Eight hours steady at a desk took some getting used to again, especially because the billing machine was different from a typewriter. It had roughly the same keyboard, but it had to be manipulated manually into various positions to accommodate the layout of the invoice sheets.

Realizing the breaking-in period was stressful, Helen steered the evening conversations away from serious and demanding topics. As they prepared vegetables for the nourishing suppers she tried to provide—aware that Claudia's tastes were adjusting remarkably well to brown bread, brown rice, and glutenburger—and as they washed up afterward, she let her sister set the tone. She listened to her chat about her new colleagues, her past ones in Lakeville, her plans with Lucky, her projects for her first paycheck. Mrs. Johnson watched her sister reread her almost daily letter from Florida—forwarded at first from Lakeville—and then go to her room. The light did not burn there long—only about time enough for an almost daily response to those letters.

Lucky. Where *did* he fit into the future that she hoped was shaping up for Claudia? Now that the Lord had answered her prayers, allowing her to witness for Him to at least one member of her family, how must she go about it? She disliked comparing herself to a serpent, but she would have to be as cunning as one, all right. As for the other part of the Bible verse about the serpent's cunning, well, she had been playing the harmless dove all week, and it had led her nowhere near the religious realm. Grace at table was the extent of their spiritual rapport. On the evenings when she had to leave for a Bible study, Claudia showed no interest in accompanying her. But Helen realized she was too impatient. She would wait on the Lord, as the Bible advised. The moment would come. Of that she felt sure.

It arrived the Friday night of Claudia's first week at work.

"M-m-m-m, it smells good in here," she said as she walked in shortly after five that Friday afternoon. "Let's see what we're having for supper. Oh, yummy, potato soup, and"—she took in the array of dishes on the deck—"apple pie and homemade rolls and some kind of casserole. You've really been cooking. And cleaning, too. Looks as if I could eat off the floor. I'm hungry enough to."

"Well, curb your appetite," Helen said. "Only the potato soup and rolls are for tonight—and canned peaches for dessert. The rest is for tomorrow noon. On Sabbath we eat our main meal then instead of in the evening, so I hope you'll be able to get home about that time."

"Oh" was all Claudia said. She hung her coat in the hall closet. "Anything I can do to help?"

"No, everything's ready. Mark's just finished his bath. He'll be out soon, and we can have our meal."

"Will I have time to press my skirt for work tomorrow before we eat? I want to get that out of my way because tonight I'm going to celebrate my first week of work. I'm going to the movies with one of the girls at work. She's going to call me and let me know if she can make it."

Taking the ironing board from the utility closet, she began to set it up.

It wasn't what Helen had hoped for, but it *was* the "moment of truth." She searched for a tactful way to phrase what she had to say. "Claudia, I'm sorry. We don't iron on Friday night. The sun is just going down and we'll have a Sabbath prayer as soon as Mark comes."

"But it's not Sabbath for *me*, Helen. *I'm* not an Adventist." Holding the ironing board half open, she looked puzzled and a little annoyed. She had to get that skirt pressed tonight. "Anyway, I thought Sabbath was Saturday, not Friday."

"It's from sundown Friday to sundown Saturday." Helen wished her husband would come and back her up. She felt uncomfortable and bossy and inarticulate. "And the Bible says that during the Sabbath hours 'thou shalt not do any work; thou, nor thy son, nor thy daughter, thy manservant, nor thy maidservant . . . nor thy stranger that is within thy gates.' "

"Where do *I* fit into that roll call?" Claudia stood the ironing board against the wall and flopped down in a chair, frustrated.

"Well, a sister isn't exactly a stranger, but you *are* 'within the gate' as a sort of . . ." Helen searched for an appropriate word. Not an outsider, that wouldn't do. Not an unbeliever. ". . . as a sort of onlooker. The same thing that would apply to a stranger applies to you, I think."

Saying nothing, Claudia put the ironing board back in the closet. She would have to work out other living arrangements sooner than she planned. She had hoped for a few weeks' grace in which to get on her financial feet, but if this sort of thing was going to happen on Friday nights . . .

At that moment the telephone rang, ending the awkward silence.

"It's for you, Claudia. Jan somebody." Helen handed her the phone.

"Hello, Jan. What about the . . . Oh, she is? . . . You can't . . . Yes, of course. I understand. We'll do it next week. Plan on it. See you Monday." Claudia hung up. "Well, there go my plans for tonight."

Shrugging, she excused herself. Helen went to the kitchen, and Mark joined her there. She told him about the ironing-board incident.

"Did I do the right thing, Mark? Should I have let her go ahead and press her skirt?"

"No. It was best to have an understanding right from the start," he answered. "It'll turn out all right. Don't worry. Let's have worship and eat. I'm starving."

Claudia, emerging from her room in her dressing gown, paused on her way toward the bathroom. "Go ahead and eat without me. I'm going to shower first. I'll feel more like eating then. Do you mind?"

"No, Claudia, that's fine." Her sister tried to keep her voice from reflecting the letdown she felt. Was the shower a ploy to avoid Sabbath prayers? To Mark she said, "Let's have worship. I think I spoiled my chance to help Claudia 'call the Sabbath a delight.' "

Worship delayed their meal long enough for Claudia to join them at table shortly after the blessing. She made no reference to the problem of ironing her skirt. "This soup is as good as Mom's, Helen. I love it. You know, I'm disappointed about Jan not being able to go with me tonight. I don't want to go alone, so I'll just forget it, I guess."

"I feel bad, Claudia. You don't want to go out alone, and we're leaving you home alone." Mrs. Johnson looked as sorry as she felt.

"Say, that's right, you're going to some kind of meeting, aren't you?"

"Yes." Helen hesitated. Should she invite her to go, too? Was *this* the moment? No, not after the way she had muffed her lines on the Sabbath subject. "I hope you won't mind. It's too bad, but we just have to attend."

"And 'strangers within the gate' aren't allowed at the meeting?" Claudia looked expectantly at them. After all, they had told her it was a *young* people's meeting. Not exactly her idea of a Friday night fling, but it would be someplace to go. She wouldn't have minded staying home and reading, but she had read almost everything on hand—except the Bibles and all the religious books and papers lying handy. Besides, she admitted to herself, she was still downright curious about how many young people—as her sister called them—would be there.

"Oh, Claudia, you'd be *more* than welcome. No such thing as a stranger at church," Helen said, not bothering to hide her surprise.

"You sure are," Mark chimed in. "And we'd better get going. Can't sit here eating all evening." He pushed back from the table and carried his dishes to the sink. "Come on, girls; time's a-wasting."

\* \* \*

## IN RETROSPECT: THE WAY IT ALL HAPPENED

Helen badly wanted Claudia's reaction to the meeting they had just attended. Deliberately not referring to it as they rode home, she herself talked casually about the blustery weather, the little ping in the engine she'd been hearing lately (did Mark think something serious was wrong?), the new baby they had heard about after meeting—waiting, hoping all the while something would lead to a comment on the speaker of the evening. Or even just the music, which had been especially good, she thought. But Claudia sat wordless in the back seat.

Had Helen been able to see her sister's face, she would have noticed total preoccupation, a mind unaware of weather, engine pings, new babies. Shortly before they arrived home, she burst out, "I just can't believe it."

"Believe what, Claudia?" both Mark and Helen said together.

"Oh, the teenagers there, and kids my age. Not to mention all those older ones in their 30s and 40s. Why, I saw people who must have even been 50 or 60! I thought you said it was a young people's meeting."

"Well, it was, really. That is, it's their program, but all ages are welcome, and they usually turn out in numbers for tonight's speaker. He's a ministerial student at our college in Valley Springs. But he's been preaching for years. Used to be known as the 'boy evangelist.' " She paused, then ventured, "What did you think of him?"

"Is he good-looking!" Claudia answered.

"That pretty blonde girl on the front row was his wife," Mark put in.

"Oh, don't worry, Mark. I'm not interested that way. Lucky is my choice." She wondered what her boyfriend would think if he knew someone had finally gotten her inside a church. "By the way, I've heard of that college in Valley Springs. It's only twenty miles from Lakeville. George told me about it when I was staying in Lakeville. He used to do some kind of business with the furniture factory at the college." She giggled. "Called the people 'peanut eaters.' "

It was Helen's turn to lapse into silence. Before those who had part in the program went onto the rostrum, she had told them about Claudia. They had special prayer that God's Spirit would touch her heart. The whole theme of the sermon was oriented to the love of God and the sacrifice of Jesus, just for her benefit. And here she was, joking about peanut eaters.

Mark was not ready to give up, however. "I thought the violinist did a great job, didn't you, girls? He's a college student, Claudia, and so's the accompanist. In fact, Helen's got a speaker and special music from the college lined up for every Friday night for a while."

Neither expected Claudia to seize that bait, but they were pleased when she carried on further about the meeting as they got out of the car and went into the house. "I wish I could play an instrument like that. I've always wanted piano lessons. Maybe someday." She hung her coat in the closet and handed Helen a hanger. "You said some of the young people weren't at the meeting tonight. Well, there must have been a half dozen there, and that's a crowd for a church, isn't it? Why do you think the others didn't come?"

"Most of them are at academy—that's high school, you know—or college right now. But when spring break comes, they'll be home, and I hope to have some of them on my program that week."

Claudia yawned and stretched. "I'm tired. It's been a long week, and I still have tomorrow morning ahead of me. But just think, Sunday morning I'll be able to sleep in. Good night, you two."

She went to bed but not immediately to sleep. Things that she had heard from someone not much older than herself ran through her mind. She remembered the only time she had even come close to the feeling she had while listening to the sermon. Just like now, she had been lying awake back home in Chesterfield—before she ever went to Lakeville and met Lucky—looking out at the starry night. Suddenly she had had a strange, exhilarating feeling of identity with a great Creative Power, with the Maker of all those stars. She remembered breathing a kind of prayer: "If You would just show me what is the truth about Yourself, I think I would follow it."

That experience had all but slipped from her memory until this evening at the meeting. Was God trying to show her truth here in River Bend, in Helen and Mark's home, in a *Seventh-day Adventist church?* She buried her head in her pillow. "Go to sleep, Claudia," she told herself. "Seven A.M. will be here before you know it."

* * *

"Lunch dishes all done, Helen. I feel such a martyr, I want you to be sure to notice." Claudia hung up the towel and poured herself a glass of juice as a reward.

"Thanks a lot, Claud. I really appreciate your doing them. I fully intended to get there before you finished, but I got too involved here."

"Sure, sure," her sister teased between swallows of juice. "I know all about dish-dodging maneuvers. I am an expert at that myself."

"Could you help me a minute in here, please?" Helen's voice now came from an odd angle. Claudia hurried to see where she was.

"Well, what have we here?" she asked, taking in the fact that Mrs. Johnson was standing on a chair struggling with a window blind that had obviously gotten out of control. The rest of the blinds were drawn and the room half darkened as a result. On the table sat a projector, its light beamed at a sheet hung on the wall at the other end of the room. "Are we going to have a Sunday morning matinee?"

"Well, not exactly. It's not a movie, but it *is* a film—a filmstrip, that is. That's the projector I use to give illustrated Bible lessons. But here, climb up. You're smaller than I am. The chair's rather wobbly. I'll get down and hold it for you. It'll be safer that way."

"You mean it will hurt *you* less if *I* fall." She took her sister's place and stretched to reach the pull cord wound around the roller. "Got it! With a little bit of luck, down we go!"

As she drew the blind, the room became almost completely dark, except for a few persistent streaks of light that edged around the blinds and under the door. Motes of dust danced in the beam of light.

"Well, all you need now is an usher," she said, getting down. "Sorry, I already have a job. But I *am* available on Saturday and Sunday."

"Don't call us, we'll call you," Helen joked. Quickly turning serious, she continued, "I'm afraid this is going to put you out of business for a while, in this room at least. Do you have something to do in your room—like writing another letter to Lucky, maybe? I've got to get ready for two appointments tomorrow, and I don't dare wait any longer."

"I don't function very well at the last minute either," Claudia said, making no move to leave the room. Instead she stood watching Helen deftly manipulate a filmstrip into the projector.

"How about your washing? You could get that done downstairs while I'm at this." Helen was relieved that her sister had not even mentioned washing the day before during Sabbath hours. After the incident with the ironing board, she had apparently caught on.

"On *Sunday?* That'll be a new twist for me. Not that it matters. But I think I'll wait till later. You might have something you want to throw in, too."

Bringing the film into focus on a Bible text subtitle, Helen then ran it through without pausing, colored pictures, diagrams, texts flashing on and off the sheet like scenery seen through a moving train window. At last she stopped, leaving in focus a giant statue of a man. His head was bright gold, his chest silver, his legs dark.

"Talk about fearfully and wonderfully made!" Claudia remembered Mark's reading those words from the Bible while they were having devotions that morning. She had heard it all from her room. "What in the world is he supposed to represent?"

"That, my ever-curious sister, is the history of the world clear down to the end of time, embodied in the statue of a man."

"So the world is going to end. Who says?"

"The Bible. The Lord."

"Where does old 'Goldilocks' come in?"

Helen thought of Jesus' words, "I will make you fishers of men." She now had her sister on the line, but tenuously. Somehow she must not let her get away! Studiously knitting her brow, she said, "It's a bit hard to give you that answer in twenty-five words or less. But I could explain it as I went through the film. That way I'd get the practice for my study and you'd get the answer. All right?"

"You can practice on me a few minutes," Claudia said, settling down in a chair where she could see the screen. "But I warn you, I've been known to walk out on films I don't like."

Claudia did not walk out. Instead she sat for an hour that flew by in what seemed half the time, looking, listening, occasionally interrupting with questions and comments. History had always been one of her favorite subjects in school. As Helen talked about Nebuchadnezzar and the kingdom of Babylon represented by the head of gold, she recalled something about it from her ancient history class in high school.

"I think there were some gardens in Babylon—hanging gardens—one of the Seven Wonders of the World, weren't they?"

"The whole city was a wonder." Claudia's obvious interest in history provided Helen with a key to holding her attention, one she decided to capitalize on. "It was laid out in a perfect square, surrounded by high walls with many brass gates in them. And it had a marvelous temple to a heathen god and two palaces with a tunnel under the River Euphrates connecting them."

"Boy, back then that must have been impressive."

"It's no surprise that the Lord chose the most precious metal to represent Babylon."

"I studied about one king—what was his name? The one that made the code of rules. Hammurabi, I think. But the name Nebuchadnezzar sounds familiar, too."

"Did you know that Nebuchadnezzar became a follower of the true God?"

"How do you know?" Up to now Claudia had accepted what Helen had said. But, remembering that Babylon was a center of astrology, she became openly skeptical.

"The book of Daniel tells about it. You see, there's more to that book than just the story of this great image found in the second chapter.

"All I know about Daniel is that the king put him in a lions' den. I guess that story would be in the same book."

"Yes, it is. But it wasn't Nebuchadnezzar who did it. In fact, he was so impressed with Daniel, he made him his minister of state. Yet, on the other hand, he was so impressed with his own dream he decided to foil Daniel's prediction of history."

"What did he do?"

"He made an image like the one in his dream, only *all* gold—like his own kingdom—and commanded people to bow down and worship it."

"Did Daniel?"

"Well, Daniel must have been out of the country, probably on some of the king's business. But three Hebrew companions of his were there and they refused to bow down. Nebuchadnezzar had them thrown into a blazing furnace."

"Oh ho! Shadrach, Meshach, and Abednego, right? I've heard a spiritual sung about that business. They got out of the furnace all right—at least according to the song."

"And accordng to the Bible, too. Later, Nebuchadnezzar went completely mad, recovered, and gave his heart to God. You can read about it in Daniel 4."

"If I can find Daniel in the Bible. I found Corinthians the other day," she confessed, "looking for that pun about charity. Is Daniel anywhere near there?"

"No, it's in the New Testament. Daniel is in the Old. But let's continue here. In the fifth chapter we read about how Belshazzar, Nebuchadnezzar's grandson, gave a great feast while Cyrus, the king of Medo-Persia besieged the city. Everyone felt safe, not knowing the Medes and Persians would divert the River Euphrates and enter the city on the dry riverbed. While the Babylonians were feasting and reveling, a hand appeared out of nowhere and wrote a message on the wall: "Mene, mene, tekel, upharsin.' "

"Sounds mysterious and scary. Did they know what it meant?"

"They didn't, not even the magicians and astrologers. So they called in Daniel—old and venerable by this time—and he told them the plain truth. Babylon would be overthrown. The golden kingdom would give way to one of silver, Medo-Persia."

Continuing on through the film, Helen explained the overthrow of Persia by Greece, the belly and thighs of brass, which in turn Rome, the legs of iron, supplanted. Claudia listened enthralled, recalling her studies of the battles that were the turning points in the rise and fall of each empire.

The toes of the image that would not cleave together, she learned, were the countries of Western Europe, fragmented, often at war with one another. The climax of the film left Claudia silent and contemplative. The stone that was "cut out of the mountain without hands" and broke in pieces the gold and silver, the brass and iron—no history book ever told *that* story.

She read the Scripture verse projected on the screen: " 'And in the days of these kings shall the God of heaven set up a kingdom, which shall never be destroyed.' According to this, I would have to say we are in the toes of time!" Playing with words came easily to her but this was no mere figure of speech. She paused as she reflected on this thought.

"Well, it seems to me," she continued, struck by a new idea, "this account leaves out one very important country. The good old U.S.A.!"

"It's true that Daniel 2 doesn't mention the United States, or any other of the great world powers, for that matter. But then it doesn't pretend to take in the whole world. It deals with what was to become the Christian world of Western Europe. While these powers are still in existence, Christ will come."

"Does this mean that the United States is not especially important to the development of what you've been calling 'God's plan'?"

"Not at all. In fact, in Revelation you can find a direct reference to America. It is called a lamblike beast, speaking with great authority, much involved with inflicting the mark of the beast."

"Really! Where's Revelation?" Claudia picked up the Bible and moved to the circle of light shed by the projector bulb.

Helen realized that so many ideas and texts, totally new to her sister, would be confusing and unconvincing. Moreover, she intended to keep her line baited. "That is a later subject we don't have time for now, Claud. We'd better get our washing done now."

Claudia blinked as Helen raised the blinds. "We cinema fans call that ending a 'cliff hanger,' " she joked. "But I thought you had *two* lessons to give tomorrow. Or do you give the same one to two different groups?"

"No. I'm doing Daniel 2 in the afternoon, and in the evening I'll be studying the question 'Is There Life After Death?' "

"Maybe . . ." Claudia hesitated. "Maybe I could go with you tomorrow night if you don't mind." She had read some things recently about communication with the dead. And Lucky had told her his grandma was now in heaven. She wanted to see what the Adventists had to say about that.

"Oh, you're welcome to come along, Claudia," Helen said, trying not to appear too eager. So far, so good. The Holy Spirit was at work, she knew. "Help me to cooperate," she prayed silently.

\* \* \*

"You know, Helen," Claudia said, as she and her sister put the projector and accompanying paraphernalia back into the trunk of the car, "I agree with you about the state of the dead. I've always been dubious about the soul going to heaven at once when a person dies—or to the other place, either one."

Appealing again to Claudia's interest in history, Helen answered, "The Greeks are the ones who taught Western man that the soul is immortal. Certainly God's Word makes no such claim, as you saw in tonight's study. There, I think everything's stowed away. Let's head for home; it's nearly ten o'clock."

Riding homeward, Claudia commented, "The Halls certainly seemed impressed tonight."

"I'm hoping they'll remain open to these Bible teachings. After all, it isn't my ability but the conviction of God's Spirit that will lead anyone who is honest in heart."

"Well, I like to think I'm honest in heart"—Claudia was remembering the night she had promised the stars that she would accept truth if God would show it to her—"But I'm not sure I'm ready to be led in the direction you take. The Sabbath, for instance. Isn't that deliberately making trouble for yourself—marching out of step with the whole world?"

"The whole world, except millions of Muslims, who observe Friday as a holy day, and thousands of Jewish people, whose holy day is Saturday, like mine. Not to mention untold billions of Oriental peoples and heathen, who keep no day at all."

"I guess I took in a little too much territory, didn't I?" Claudia giggled at her rashness. "I should start over and limit myself to Christendom, right? In which case, you're still out of step, so touché!"

"But to be out of step with one's conscience and with *God* would be even worse, to my mind."

Her sister thought a moment. "Well, if you're going to bring Him into it, I was quite conservative, after all. If God keeps your Sabbath, then the whole universe, except mankind, does as well. Do you think so?"

"At least He planned that kind of cycle for man's world, and someday, we'll observe it with Him in heaven as He did at Creation in the beginning."

"But how do you know Saturday is the day that He kept in the beginning? Hasn't the calendar been juggled around a lot?"

"I mentioned the Jewish people a while back. The same weekly cycle has gone through their history from the beginning. Did you know that?"

"Actually, I don't know much about the Jews. Do they really go to church on Saturday?"

"The Orthodox ones attend synagogue—their sanctuary—on Saturday. Of course many of them have given up their religious practices. Just like many nonpracticing Christians, who know the significance of their religious heritage, such as Christmas and Easter, for instance."

"But still, Helen, think of all the important people in the world who observe Sunday. What Jew is as influential as the pope, for example?"

"I can think of one very important Person, Jewish by birth and far more influential than the pope, who kept the Sabbath."

"Who?" Tantalized by Helen's methods, Claudia awaited the answer eagerly.

"Jesus."

"Are you sure He did?"

"The Bible says so."

"As we say in the movies, 'this is where I came in.' I heard that line—'the Bible says'—a lot tonight."

"And this is where we'd both better *go* in! Do you realize how long we've been sitting here in the driveway since we got home? You're going to hate getting up tomorrow morning, so no more talk for now. I'm going to give a study on the question of the Sabbath to the Harding family Thursday night. Want to come along?"

\* \* \*

Claudia lay in bed wide awake the following Thursday night, her mind reeling with new concepts she never dreamed existed before she came to stay with Helen and Mark. It was one thing to feel moved by the appeal of the young evangelist at the meeting Friday night, to want to say,

"Take me, Jesus, 'just as I am,' I'm Yours." But the strange new doctrines that she had been hearing from Helen were something else. Yet they seemed so *right*.

She had certainly not intended to get involved this way. How had it happened, anyway? She recited to herself the steps by which she had become more and more involved, in spite of herself, it seemed. First, she herself had made the initial move, by going to the Friday night meeting. There she had been touched by the story of the love of God for His lost sheep—with whom she had suddenly, inexplicably identified.

Then she had sat through the study on Daniel 2, fascinated by the history of the nations. Next, she had had confirmed her belief that the end of life was the grave, not limbo or purgatory or heaven—not at once, anyway. She herself had arranged to attend that lesson.

And now tonight, drawn by what magnet she could not say, she had gone with Helen to the lesson on the Sabbath and had come away thoroughly discomfited. How could she change her whole life pattern, what could she do about her work on Saturday mornings—if in the end she decided that observing Sabbath was paramount?

When sleep finally released her from the mental acrobatics she had been performing, her dreams were of a great golden-headed image threatening to kick her with his iron foot right into a burning fiery furnace if she didn't go to church on Saturday!

The next night, once again, she attended the young people's meeting. There a young man from Valley Springs told the story of his conversion, of giving up a promising career in major league baseball to study for the ministry. Once again the starry-night experience washed over her: the tug on the heart, the inner feeling of love that was nothing like what she felt for Lucky.

When they arrived home and were relaxing in the living room with their shoes kicked off, the peaceful Sabbath atmosphere continued to warm her heart. Claudia wanted to talk on about the meeting, about the ministerial student's experience, about the way she felt.

Mark yawned and dozed as they chatted. Finally he gave up. "I've got to turn in. After a hard week at the plant, I'm no good on Friday night except to rest. The Lord knew what He was doing when He made the Sabbath for man."

"That echoes a Bible text, you know, Claud," Helen was quick to say, as they bade Mark good night. "A good text coming from Mark—because in Mark 2:27, Jesus said, 'The sabbath was made for man, and not man for the sabbath.' "

"Hold it, Helen. I remember Dad using those very words to prove that you were off the track insisting on keeping the seventh day. He said God set aside the day for man's good, so any day served the purpose and that you 'Advents' were twisting it instead so that it seemed *man* was made for the *Sabbath.*"

"Well, it seems to me that Jesus was saying in the context of this verse that the many picayune rules and regulations on the observance of the Sabbath that some Jews had made resulted in its being a burden instead of the blessing He meant it to be.

"You know," she continued, "they had carefully measured out the limits of a Sabbath day's journey—about two thirds of a mile. To go beyond that was to break the Sabbath. They restricted writing to *two* letters of the alphabet. They forbade tying or loosening a knot, lighting or putting out a fire. Why, they couldn't even carry a handkerchief unless an end of it was attached to the clothes so that one could consider it clothing!"

"Was it safe to breathe?"

"I'm not sure! No wonder Jesus emphasized that the Sabbath was made for man's benefit, not to his detriment. It wasn't simply a Jewish institution, but something meant for the good of mankind in general. In fact, it preceded the Jewish race by many centuries."

Claudia yawned and stretched. "I'll have to admit I think it's a good idea to put aside your work and worries once a week and forget everything."

"Everything except what we are commanded to remember in the fourth commandment."

"Which is?"

"To honor the seventh day in commemoration of God's creative power, both in nature and in our lives."

"Somewhere since the time God gave the Ten Commandments, somebody switched something around. You didn't get into that at the study Thursday night."

"Well, it wasn't the Jews. Here"—Helen pulled a magazine from the bookcase—"listen to this: 'Throughout the ages the Sabbath has been . . . the protecting institution of the Jewish people. It has been a day not only of physical rest but of spiritual recreation. The Sabbath is the strength of the Jewish people.'

"These are the words of a Jewish rabbi quoted in our church paper."

"My, I didn't know they felt so strongly about the Sabbath," Claudia said. "But then, as I mentioned the other day, I didn't really know anything about their beliefs and customs. Anyway, if they didn't do it, then who did?"

"It wasn't Jesus. He said, 'Think not that I am come to destroy the law, or the prophets.' In fact, He declared that He had come to fulfill, or establish, the law, and that not 'one jot or one tittle' would pass from it until all was fulfilled—which has not happened yet."

"Well, at least I'm finding out who it *wasn't!*"

"It wasn't the apostles, either. There are, I think, at least eighty-four recorded Sabbath meetings of the apostles with the church in the New Testament. I can give you the texts."

"I'll take your word for it, Helen. You win! But I still don't know who *changed* things. According to Dad, Sunday is as good a day as any because Jesus was resurrected on that day."

"And what did Jesus do on the day before, on the Sabbath day? He *rested* in the tomb. Why, the women wouldn't even put the spices on His body until the Sabbath was over—which says He didn't leave them any information about a change to take place after His death."

"But it seems to me that His resurrection is important

enough for something like Sunday to commemorate it."

"Jesus Himself left us two ordinances—sacraments, if you will—in memory of His death and resurrection: baptism and Communion. The Bible tells us about both. But it's getting late now, and we need to get to bed. We'll talk more about them tomorrow afternoon, if you wish."

"Along with who turned Sabbath into Sunday—the question you still have not answered?" Claudia could see that her sister was deliberately holding back some answers to lead her on, but somehow it didn't matter. She was learning so many new things she felt almost as if she had landed on another planet. It was, well, interesting, to say the least, and, at times, *very* disturbing.

* * *

During the weeks that followed, Claudia found her life so full she had little time to miss Lucky or to count days until his return. It amused her, when she thought of it, how tragic their separation had seemed when they parted, how long the six months had loomed ahead. In fact, time had passed almost too quickly. She had hardly enough of it in her busy days to write to him!

After work, two or three evenings a week, she went with Helen to her Bible studies. Both now accepted her going as routine. She would help load into the car the projector, Bibles, religious publications, health foods, little gifts for the children in the homes they visited, and whatever else Helen took each time.

After carrying her share of it into the house, she would take her place in what she called the "amen section." She would read aloud the texts from the screen at the appropriate times and look them up in the Bible when those attending wanted to see them actually in print. (Already she had learned where many of them were located.) And she even found herself answering some of the questions posed by "Helen's people."

Claudia still had many of her own questions to ask, and on Sabbath afternoons—what an easy habit to acquire, calling Saturday Sabbath—on Sundays, or evenings when the Johnsons had no outside study scheduled, she and Helen had further discussions that usually led to an organized quest for texts on a particular subject.

Lucky's letters she quickly wrote in spare moments, with no mention of her religious activities. Time would come for that later. It did limit her subject matter considerably, however, and she wondered if he might be asking himself, as he read her quick missives, if she ever did anything besides work! Well, he would see one of these days!

A Sabbath came in early April when she had run out of questions about who changed it to Sunday—she had learned that not only from Helen and the Bible but from books by those who claimed responsibility for it. Nor had she any further queries about why it was important and how it would figure in the closing events of time. She dressed slowly and mechanically, deeply preoccupied with a weighty decision she must make this very morning.

"Hurry, Claud! It's after eight. There's not much time to get you to the bank and ourselves to the church by nine fifteen." The voice of her sister penetrated her consciousness and roused her to action.

"Coming," she answered, assuming a tone far more cheerful than her inner turmoil warranted. With a last quick look in the mirror, she ran out the door and into the car waiting outside.

As her brother-in-law drove across town, Claudia was scarcely aware of the conversation that eddied around her. She was too busy memorizing a speech she would soon make to a one-man audience—her boss.

Mark drew up to the curb in front of the Fidelity Bank building.

"Do you think you could . . . would you mind waiting for me a few minutes?" she began. Then, with conviction, "I'm not working today. I'm going to church with you."

"*Mind!* Oh, Claudia," Helen exulted, "for this we'd be willing to be late! We've been praying you would make this decision. We're thrilled, aren't we, Mark?"

Already half out of the car, she did not hear his answer.

*LUCKY IN LOVE*

Into the building she hurried, in and out of the elevator, and down the familiar second-floor corridor. As she approached her employer's office, her steps slowed and butterflies began to wing around in her stomach. Then she brightened. Maybe Mr. Berry would not be in. He seldom arrived this early. She would leave a note on his desk and make her getaway. By Monday, after thinking over her request for Saturdays off, he would probably be quite mellow. How could he refuse her a few hours on Saturday morning, especially if she offered to stay an extra hour each of the other five days? Pleased with the logic of it all, she opened the door—and there sat Mr. Berry at his desk!

One thing she was thankful for as she emerged a few minutes later—the ordeal had not lasted long. It came back to her vividly as she hurried down the hall—the shy, stammering way she had addressed her boss, her hesitation, her half-whispered reference to going to church. She still felt a little weak-kneed as she remembered the stern look on Mr. Berry's face and the forbidding tone of his voice, reminding her that he had warned her about this when he had hired her and that she had been at the job only about three months. Who was she to ask for special privileges, didn't she realize that everyone else would want Saturday off, and now that they'd just nicely broken her in they'd have to let her go?

"We'll put your check in the mail," he had said.

As she got into the car and announced that she was now free to go to church, Helen could not contain her surprise. "You mean Mr. Berry is actually letting you be absent from work on Saturday?" she asked incredulously.

"Yes," her sister replied, her eyes betraying the half-truth her lips had uttered. "As a matter of fact, he told me I could also be absent every day of the week. Well, what are we waiting for? Let's go to church!"

* * *

The warm welcome she received when they arrived at church surprised and touched Claudia. Here she was, unemployed at a time when jobs were few, and people were

50

congratulating her as if she had just had a promotion and welcoming her into the fold like a lost sheep. Well, she was a lost sheep, she knew that. But she also knew that she had found the Shepherd—or, rather, He had found her. And so she kept her first Sabbath and was able to call it a delight.

The following day, however, was traumatic enough to efface, almost, the happiness of the Sabbath experience.

"Will you tell Dad about your decision to become an Adventist, Claud?" Helen asked as they got into the car for the sixty-mile drive to Chesterfield.

"I'm not sure. This will be the last time I will see the folks before they move West, and I hate to upset them, especially Dad. He was never pleased about your joining the church. Why is he so anti-Adventist?"

"Well, you know he's always been against churches of any kind. To him, organized religion is the mark of the beast. If you listened to him, you'd think the Adventist Church was the beast itself." Helen paused, reflecting on her own experience with their father. "And," she went on, "don't forget, you are his special little beauty. He wouldn't want you, of all people, to fall into the claws of the beast. Yes, today's farewell to the folks is a very delicate matter. Pray for tact."

All the way to Chesterfield, the problem of her father distracted Claudia. To tell or not to tell, that was her question. She had not settled on the answer when they turned into their parents' drive. Nor did the subject arise while they helped with some of the packing and, perched on cartons and crates, had their lunch. It was almost time to leave in late afternoon when Dad made the remark that triggered the upsetting episode that followed.

"You haven't said a thing today about your work, Claudia. Mr. Berry still expecting clean carbon copies of every invoice?"

"I'm . . . I'm not working at the bank anymore, Dad. I couldn't get Sabbath off."

"Sabbath *off!*" Mr. Foster roared, his eyes blazing. "You joining those Advent freaks too? Have you lost your mind?"

"No, Dad, I haven't. In fact, I believe I've only just found it."

"You look here, young lady," her father shouted, his face livid, "you and I have just come to the parting of the ways. You think it's smart to go off on some fanatical tangent the first chance you get? Well, you needn't bother to come home until you've got these foolish notions out of your head. You understand?" Turning on his heel, he stormed out of the room.

The drive back to River Bend was silent and strained. Recalling the reaction of their father and the tears and hand-wringing of their mother as they parted, no one felt like saying much. Helen searched for comforting words to offer her sister and chose those of Jesus: " 'And every one that hath forsaken houses, or brethren, or sisters, or father, or mother, . . . for my name's sake, shall receive an hundredfold, and shall inherit everlasting life' (Matt. 19:29)."

Still reeling from her lost job and ruptured family relationship, Claudia did not know that a third blow still awaited her.

\* \* \*

"You're looking pretty neat, Kid Sister," Mark teased as Claudia waited for her very special Thursday evening date.

"True? Must be the unique way I blush. As a matter of fact, I'm rather nervous about seeing Lucky, after all these months."

"What will he say about your interest in joining our church?" Helen asked, an edge of apprehension in her voice. She could not bear to think of her sister being hurt again.

"Oh, he'll be dee-lighted. From the first time we met, he's been after me to go to church with him."

"But his church is not an Adventist church," Mark reminded her, "and 'keeping Saturday for Sunday' may strike him as a little unusual."

"Have you written him anything at all about the issues we've been studying these past weeks?" Helen inquired.

## IN RETROSPECT: THE WAY IT ALL HAPPENED

"No, I wanted to surprise him. Just think! Six months ago when he went to Florida, he left behind a 'little infidel'—that's what he always called me—but tonight he meets a 'true believer.' And I hope you realize," she bantered, "that it's all your fault, Helen. It was pretty sneaky of you to lure me into going with you to your Bible studies for 'company and help.' You got along without me before."

"But not very well," Helen said, assuming a properly chastened look.

"And that casual way you apologized my first night here, about leaving me alone while you went to meeting. I practically had to insist on my right to go with you that first time. Talk about religious freedom!"

The doorbell rang just then, and a glowing Claudia was swept into the arms of a tall 20-year-old with black curly hair, and after only the briefest of greetings and goodbyes, out into the balmy spring night.

Much later a subdued Claudia stood before the bedroom door her sister had deliberately left ajar. She whispered into the narrow opening, "Are you too sleepy to talk a little, Helen?"

"To tell the truth, I haven't gone to sleep yet," Helen replied, emerging in robe and slippers. "I had a premonition Lucky wouldn't be as 'dee-lighted' as you thought. I can see I was right." She pulled Claudia onto the sofa beside her. "Tell me about it."

"I guess I succeeded in surprising him, all right. In fact, I gave him a real shock. Oh, Helen," she sobbed, "I went about it all wrong—threw the whole book at him—no more movies, no dancing, no tea or coffee, no meat . . ."

"What did he say to all that, Claud?"

"He didn't say anything at first. He let me talk on and on while he only stared at me as if I'd just dropped in from Mars. Then . . . then"—it was time for more tears. Helen handed her a fresh tissue and waited while she wiped her eyes and nose. "Then he said, 'For heaven's sake, Claudia, what's happened to you? You expect me to swallow the whole Bible in one gulp, from Genesis to Revelation and promise I'll quit doing everything that's fun and start going to church with you—on Saturday, at that!' " Another burst of tears interrupted the recital.

"And then?"

"Anyway, after that, he told me I'd get over it, and I told him I never would . . . and . . . I gave him his ring back." A tear splashed on the left hand she held up with its bare fourth finger, and she managed a little laugh. "I guess I'd have taken it off, in any case—if I'm going to be a proper Seventh-day Adventist!"

# PART III

# The Rest of the Story

Lucky was unpacking boxes of nails and shelving them in Bradley's Hardware in Lakeville on a gusty December morning. The job, requiring very little concentration, allowed his mind to wander over the past few weeks since he had come home from the war. Civilian life was proving hard to get used to after almost four years in the military. Tenpenny nails didn't snap into place like those rookies he had given basic training in Arkansas for so many months. You couldn't make customers "shape up or ship out," as you could the new recruits. Instead you had to handle them gently, wheedle and cosset them, because they were "always right."

He thought of the various stages of his Army career with some nostalgia—a feeling he never thought he would have! After Arkansas came Louisiana for a brief hitch at state university, the military giving him his first taste of college life. From there into the Tenth Mountain Division, the newest branch of the Infantry, known as the ski troops, trained for mountain warfare.

Now there was a *man*'s life! Stationed in Camp Hale, nine thousand feet up in the Colorado Rockies, you found yourself bivouacking in heights far above, sleeping under the stars in your eiderdown sleeping bag, the only barrier against −35° F. temperatures. Besides downhill and cross-country skiing, alpine experts from Austria and Norway taught you to snowshoe and rock-climb, and to ski with a seventy-five-pound pack on your back.

Nothing could quite match the exhilaration you felt

standing alone at the summit of a high peak in a winter world, your own white parka, white skis, and white gun all a part of the vast whiteness. It was rugged and challenging, and—except for the fright and the danger in actual combat—much tougher than the fighting itself.

And now here he was, waiting counter, delivering appliances, sorting nails—hardly what you'd call exciting. But it earned a living while he tried to find himself, tried to ignore the prosperity of old friends who had somehow escaped Uncle Sam's long arm and had held down two defense plant jobs. He even had to deliver new refrigerators and washing machines to their well-furnished homes.

Funny how things worked out. If the war in the Pacific had ended at the same time as the one in Europe, no doubt he'd have had to remain in Italy—or go to Germany or France—with the occupying forces. Lots of the men had to stay on in one of those places after V-E Day. But when its brief, bloody stint in Italy ended, the Tenth had boarded ship to head for Japan to fight the mountain warfare there. They had been furloughed Stateside for a brief rest, and during that time the bomb had fallen on Hiroshima, and it all ended.

Already in the States, he had been mustered out and, almost before he was ready for it, found himself in civvies, in Lakeville, and in need of a job. Joe Bradley had taken him on as a vet with some retail experience (thanks to Bailey's Market, years ago), and rather dull, routine life had begun a little more than a month ago.

The door swung open, admitting a whiff of crisp December air and George Preston.

"Well, look who's here," Lucky said, shaking off his reverie and extending his hand. "It's been years, George."

"Sure has. But it's great to shake hands with a genuine hero. Maybe I should salute!"

"Come on, George, the real heroes are still over there—or," he added, remembering his fallen friends, "didn't come back at all."

It was hard to forget those battle scenes, hard to

overcome the training that had kept him on the alert, on guard, for so long. No wonder he found himself under the bed, hugging the floor, when awakened by a freight train rumbling by a few nights back.

"You know how you never have enough of them," he heard George saying.

"Enough of what, George?"

"Why, extension cords, Lucky. It's what I just asked for." George looked at him a bit quizzically. Had the war affected his hearing? Or was his faraway attitude a reaction to the quiet home front? He looked well enough, George thought; in fact, better than he'd ever seen him—husky and mature.

"Sure, sure, this way, George," Lucky said quickly, chagrined that his reminiscing had made him forget a customer.

As they walked to the back of the store, George remarked casually, "By the way, you'll never guess who's living next door to us now."

"No, who?"

"Does the name Helen or Mark Johnson mean anything to you?"

Lucky didn't have to reflect long—he had written "in care of" by that name on enough letters. "You mean they've moved over here from River Bend?"

"Uh-huh. Mark needed a job when he got out of the service on a medical discharge about a year ago, and Helen wanted to be near Gladys, so he decided to look for work here. Nice couple. Though rather extreme in some ways."

"I never really got acquainted with the Johnsons."

"Look, I think just this ordinary one will do. We only need it for the Christmas tree." George paused then, with the smug look of someone who knows something his listener doesn't, and is about to announce it. "You'll never guess who's spending Christmas with them."

Lucky almost dropped the cord he was putting into a paper bag. "Not Claudia!"

"You got it."

"So that's what brought you to Bradley's today," Lucky

joked. "You wanted to let me in on the latest. Here's your cord, anyway, man—and that'll be $1.69, please."

"To tell the truth, Lucky, I wasn't sure you'd be here. I heard you had started working for some local merchant. But, honest, it was just a coincidence that I needed a cord and found you."

"Well, thanks, George." Lucky handed him his change. "How is Claudia, anyway?"

"She's fine. She's in her last year at that peanut eaters' school in Valley Springs. Been working her way through college doing secretarial work, proofreading, editing. She's . . ." He hesitated. "She's engaged, you know."

"No, I didn't."

"That's right—I guess you wouldn't. You two split up even before you went into the Army, if I remember correctly. We don't know much about the lad she's going to marry. Studying to be a minister, I think. Same school."

"Guess she really meant what she told me about never giving up," Lucky mused.

"What's that?"

"Nothing, nothing. Good to see you again, George. Say Hello to Gladys. Back to my shelving now."

"So long, old buddy. See you around."

The door opened and closed with another cold gust, and Lucky went back to his work in a pensive mood. So Claudia was getting married. Well, what else could he expect? Life went on here in the States during the war years. Business as usual, except for the draftees. He was surprised she had waited this long. Wouldn't do any harm, would it, to drop around and wish her well?

* * *

It was a scene that could have been printed on a Christmas card—the cozy living room, the Christmas tree aglow in front of the picture window, the festively wrapped presents underneath. Helen was wrapping still more gifts in the bedroom. Mark was next door with George. Claudia, luxuriating in the idleness of the holidays, could think of nothing more tempting to do than sit staring at the lights.

"It's very quiet in there," Helen called from the bedroom. "Why not put on a Christmas record? Or are you sleeping, are you sleeping, Sister Claud?"

"No, I'm not, and the morning bells aren't ringing, either. In fact, I don't quite know how to act without class bells and alarm clocks ringing. These past few days I've been so relaxed I'm afraid I'll never get back in stride."

"You've needed this breather, Claudia." Mrs. Johnson walked into the room to add another package to the growing Christmas heap.

"I didn't realize how much, really, until I began to unwind here. It just came to me as I sat here doing nothing that this is the first time I have taken a school vacation off since I started college more than four years ago."

"That's exactly what I mean. You have stuck at your studies and your almost full-time job faithfully, and you deserve this time."

"But I couldn't have made my expenses if I hadn't worked during all the breaks."

Helen sat down on the sofa. "I know. I wish we could have helped you more." Claudia's heavy program had always worried her. But Mark's Army stint had set them back considerably. Getting established again had not been easy. An occasional item of clothing and a little spending money now and then were about all they could offer her. Well, at least she didn't have much longer now, and it was pleasant to have her with them for the holidays. Just like old times.

"You know," she said, steering the conversation to a less weighty topic, "I haven't got Mark's present yet. I wanted to give him some camera gadget, but what? The budget is too tight for much, and photographic equipment is terribly expensive. As well as scarce, yet."

"You've spent too much on me, that's why. I've seen my name on several tags."

"So you've been peeking at the packages, have you? Naughty girl!"

"I can't help it. It's my overriding vice. In fact, now that you've brought in another, I'd better see who that one is for!" She pushed herself out of the depths of her big armchair, knelt down by the tree, and picked up a red-and-silver package."

At that moment the doorbell rang.

Helen went to the door. "Well, look who's here!"

"And look who's squeezing packages under the Christmas tree," said a familiar voice. She dropped the package and rose quickly.

"Lucky Marshall!"

"Hello, Claudia," Lucky said, stamping snow off his feet and stepping into the room. "Guilty or not guilty?"

"You caught me red-handed. What else can I plead but guilty?"

The two stood looking at each other, hardly aware of the words they were exchanging.

She hasn't changed much—a lot thinner but otherwise still the same, he was thinking.

He's even better looking than before—so filled out and mature, was her instant appraisal.

"Won't you sit down, Lucky?" Helen said. "Here, let me take your jacket."

"Thanks, Mrs. Johnson. You're looking good, Claudia. How long have you been in town?"

"Just a few days. And you? I see you're not in uniform. Are you out of the Army?"

"That's right. Over a month now. I'm working at Bradley's Hardware. Your brother-in-law came in yesterday to buy something. He told me you were here."

"But what a surprise to see you!"

"You don't think I'd let you come to Lakeville without saying Hi, do you?"

Claudia had no answer. Helen filled the short silence. "I'll make us something hot to drink."

"That sounds good. It's cold and snowy outside, I can tell you."

By the time Helen returned with mugs of hot cocoa and excused herself to continue wrapping, Lucky and Claudia had found some conversational icebreaker that had led to an animated exchange.

"The day we sailed into New York Harbor," Lucky was saying, "was false V-J Day. The fire boats came out to meet our ship and gave us a royal welcome. I believe we'd have had a ticker tape parade down Fifth Avenue if they hadn't learned a little later that the Japanese hadn't surrendered after all."

"I'm so happy they didn't wait much longer before they finally did give in."

"Me, too, Claudia. There's no glamour in war, no matter what I used to think when I read Sir Walter Scott and those other romantic writers of his ilk. I certainly don't have any illusions about it now."

"I don't suppose you even care to talk about it, do you?"

"Not really. Not yet, anyway. I imagine I'll tell my grandchildren about it someday," he mused. "What about you, Claudia? George says you're graduating soon. What will you do after that?"

Here was the moment for Claudia to mention her forthcoming marriage. Instead she said, "I'm getting my secondary teaching certificate. By the way, do you still remember any French?"

She waited for his answer with interest, feeling just the least bit superior. Years before, in his conversations with her, Lucky had enjoyed using various French expressions that she, having studied Latin as her foreign language requirement in high school, couldn't understand. It had been most frustrating, she recalled. Now she would be graduating with a French major.

Lucky stood up and bowed ostentatiously. *"Si je puis vous être utile, mademoiselle, je suis entièrement à votre disposition."*

"Well! That certainly rolled off your tongue easily enough," Claudia said, trying not to show the comeuppance she felt. "Were you in France as well as Italy?"

"No. That's where I wanted to go. But Uncle Sam doesn't give a soldier much choice. In fact, when he sent me to Louisiana State, I barely missed being in a group sent to

Princeton for language study. They had put some of us through a battery of tests. I wish now I hadn't scored as high as I did on the math part. They sent me into engineering instead. In less than a year, I knew that engineering wasn't for me, even if the Army didn't! As soon as I could get out of the program, I joined up with the Tenth. Which was about as difficult to get into as LSU. It was an elite outfit."

"So I've heard. You saw some rough action, they say. And you got the Purple Heart, besides."

"Well, thanks to your prayers and my mother's, I escaped with my life. But let's not talk about me. How did you manage to get into college—financially, I mean?"

"Providentially."

"In what way?"

"I lost my job at Fidelity Trust, you know—because I . . . well, because of Sabbath." Here Claudia paused. How much did she dare go into the religious aspect this time? Still, *he* had mentioned prayers.

"And then?"

"And after looking most of the summer for a job, I took on housework for a church member to support myself. I couldn't stay forever with Mark and Helen."

"You didn't go back to Chesterfield and your folks?"

"I couldn't. That is . . ."

Somehow timid about her early experience now that the rosy glow of conversion had diminished and she had settled into the status of growing Christian, Claudia couldn't bring herself to tell him about her parents' disowning her. She finished by saying, "They don't live in Chesterfield anymore, you see. They're in Oregon."

"So you stayed in River Bend."

"Yes, and here's the providential part. At the end of the summer, I was invited one evening to the home of another church member. Her cousin was at dinner too, and he happened to be the business manager of the Adventist college in Valley Springs. He was very sympathetic to my situation. A few days later I got a letter from him asking me to come and work there in one of the offices."

"At the printshop, where I found you a year or so ago before I went overseas."

"That's right. Well, that's how I got into college. I began taking classes—a reduced load, of course—and worked."

"And worked and worked, according to George. How did you do it?"

"Classes around the edge of about five hours of work every day and ten, usually, on Sundays. Holiday vacations. Summers."

"That's rugged, Claudia. You're thinner than I've ever seen you. How did you manage to do the extra things Gladys told me about when I stopped to say Hello on the way here—such as editing the school paper and the yearbook? And getting good grades, besides."

"Come on, Lucky. Stop making such a heroine of me. Lots of my friends have done as much. The . . . the Lord has seen me through."

"Well, I personally am very proud of you. You deserve the *Légion d'Honneur!*"

*"Merci bien, monsieur. Tu es très gentil."*

"And you've picked up some French, too!"

"A little." Claudia couldn't suppress a cat-that-ate-the-cream smile. "I'll be teaching it next year, Lucky. And English."

"How about that! I knew that accent was too good to be acquired overnight. And in spite of my one memorized sentence, I think I've about forgotten all I knew of French. So please don't break into conversation."

"Don't worry. I still have a long way to go to be fluent."

"You know, I found the language background I had useful, even so. I managed to get a working knowledge of Italian while in Italy."

"Good for you!"

"Well, my accomplishments pale beside yours."

"Not at all. *You* fought a war."

"Sure. There were only 14,999 others in my outfit!"

"My own warfare has only been financial. And spiritual," she added after a moment's hesitation.

"I have a feeling you combined them. What *did* you do for cash, anyway? You couldn't pay tuition and living expenses, buy clothes, and everything on your wages, could you?"

"That's true. If you were interested, I could tell you a dozen stories of how my prayers were answered when I needed something."

"I *am* interested. You see, when I was lying in the foxholes in Italy wondering whether I'd ever get home alive, I did a lot of serious thinking. Prayer became an important part of my life, too."

Encouraged by so responsive an audience, Claudia began to talk about her years in college, of her dependence on God for support, and of His unfailing help. She steered clear of dogma this time, trying only to portray the joy of partnership with the Lord. Lucky's relaxed company made her feel comfortable and at ease. He interjected questions, comments, war anecdotes. Their usual humor and repartee spiced the serious conversation. It was almost as if five years had not elapsed since they first met and more than a year since their last brief encounter. Except—how different they were now, how widely their paths had diverged!

Suddenly it was almost midnight. Mark had slipped in through the kitchen door, and he and Helen had disappeared down the hall, unnoticed. Claudia looked at her watch. "I can't believe how late it is! I came to Lakeville to get some rest, Lucky. You always did play havoc with my bedtime hours," she chided with mock severity.

"Sorry. I'll be going. I'm older now and wiser. If you'll let me come back tomorrow night, I promise not to stay beyond ten or ten-thirty."

Claudia did not answer immediately. She was, after all, engaged. Was it proper? Still, they had only had a friendly chat, with many spiritual overtones. Didn't she owe it to Lucky to witness from her more mature perspective, without overwhelming him with Adventist do's and don'ts?

"I accept your promise, Lucky. Promptly at ten o'clock I'll probably turn into a pumpkin."

"OK, Cinderella. Good night."

\* \* \*

Helen was concerned. Right now Claudia was waiting for the arrival of Lucky Marshall with almost as much anticipation, it seemed, as for a first date. That morning she had washed and pin-curled her hair as if she had not just gone through that rather tedious process only yesterday. After that, she had made a thoughtful selection from her slender wardrobe of an outfit to wear in the evening, and even before lunchtime she was already biding her time. Was her interest in an "old flame" rekindling?

Mrs. Johnson tried to dismiss the thought. Claudia was no longer a high school girl, after all. She knew the restrictions her engagement put on her relationship with young men. And even if social custom didn't demand such propriety, Claudia's conscience would—of that she felt sure.

No, her concern was not so much with that aspect of the visit as it was with the fact that Lucky was no nearer now to Claudia's strict Christian standards than he was four years back. He was, in fact, probably a little further removed. Didn't she detect an odor of tobacco about him last night when she took his jacket? Surely Claudia must have noticed it. And yet—well, without question, he was a most charming fellow, and her sister couldn't help being attracted to him again.

Finally Helen told herself that she would have to pray especially this evening that Claudia's good sense would prevail. With great determination she had just begun to reread a page she hadn't turned for the last fifteen minutes in the book she was holding when Mark called from his basement darkroom. She laid down the book. No doubt he wanted her to see his latest prints.

At the same time Claudia emerged from her room, freshly combed and casually but carefully dressed in skirt and sweater, a subtle fragrance of powder and cologne accompanying her. She sat down on the sofa and picked up the book Helen had left on the coffee table. It lay unopened in her lap as she studied the Christmas lights, then her fingernails, then her watch. Strange, she thought, that Lucky hadn't come yet. Already it was after eight o'clock. At this rate, they wouldn't have a very long visit, and she had thought of some interesting ways to lead into a discussion of life in the new earth—a subject bound to make him as attracted to eternity as she was. But she determined to abide by the curfew, no matter what.

Lucky still had not come when Mark and Helen came upstairs a little later. Claudia's head—copper-highlighted in the glow of the lamp—was studiously bent over her book, so neither commented on the delayed visit. They went into the kitchen and clothes-pinned onto a little line above the sink the glossies Mark had fished from their bath. Then they telephoned neighbors George and Gladys to come for a view. Eric's tall preteen frame was prominent in one of them, Jennifer and her mother in another.

Soon the four sat around the kitchen table, discussing the pictures, the news of the day, the state of the post-war world. At some point in their conversation, Helen's attentive ear heard the door open and close in the living room and subdued voices thereafter, one of them a deep bass. Lucky had come. Over a warm drink, the two couples continued their visit until someone yawned and someone else commented that ten o'clock came around very fast and wasn't it about bedtime? Gladys and George were getting up to leave when the kitchen door swung open, and Claudia entered— flushed and rather sober, Helen thought.

"Mind if I join you?"

"We were just leaving," George announced. "But we may hang around a minute or two—to get the latest on Lucky. He never used to leave this early a few years back!"

Claudia tried to smile. "No, this time he had a deadline. And he barely got here before it was time to leave. So we had a little visit—and he left."

She didn't seem inclined to say more just then. After a few minutes of casual conversation, Gladys said, "We really must go, George. We'll appreciate those prints when they're dry, Mark. It's great to have a photographer in the family."

After they had said Good night to the Prestons, Claudia lingered at the table. It seemed a signal that she wanted to talk. Mark and Helen sat down again. "How's Lucky tonight?" Mark asked, sensing that his sister-in-law needed an opener.

"Not so great. I'm really disappointed, in fact. Do you know, it was almost nine when he got here?"

"Did he say why he was so late?" Helen asked.

"Well, he apologized and said he had run into a high school friend who's just out of the Army, too. He said, 'Of course we had to talk awhile.' And I said, 'And have a few drinks.' "

"So that's it. He'd been drinking. You could tell?" Mark asked.

"Of course. When he talked, his breath gave him away."

"Was he . . . was he drunk?" Helen wanted to know.

"Oh, no. I'm sure all he had was the usual 'social drink.' But to someone as unaccustomed to alcohol as I am, it was rather upsetting. Especially because he knows how I have always felt about drinking. And he never used to drink—or smoke either. Admittedly he began both in the good old U.S. Army.

"Don't feel too bad, Claudia," Helen said. "He is no different, after all, from others his age. It's you who are different. Not many conform to your standards."

"I know. But he seemed so sensitive to spiritual things last night, and I had great ideas about leading him into talking about . . . oh well . . . it's no use."

Helen and Mark listened sympathetically as she aired her letdown feelings. "Lucky just wasn't ready tonight," Helen said.

"I know one thing—this is the second time I've struck out trying to interest him in my church. And furthermore," Claudia declared as she strode purposefully from the room blinking back tears of frustration, "it's the last time I'm going to have anything to do with Lucky Marshall—*ever!*"

\* \* \*

The winter months passed quickly for Claudia. She had no time in the pressures of teaching duties—some for practice teaching credit, some for a few important weekly dollars—to let the gloom of January and February bother her, or to notice March mud and April sogginess. More pressures built up in May, compounded by a lowered resistance to spring fever. She kept up the pace, however, until June brought relief and the weekend so long awaited.

"At last, at long last," Claudia told herself as she put on her academic robe in front of the mirror and squared her mortarboard firmly on her forehead. "This is not the most flattering hat I've ever worn," she commented to her roommate.

"But it *is* one of the most expensive!" Beth replied, adjusting her own. "Is the tassel worn on the right or the left?"

"We'll see when we get into line. I always forget. You know, Beth, my college class is less than the size of my high school one. Little Chesterfield was fortunate to dredge up fifty of us, but Valley Springs has come up with only thirty-seven."

"Well, the war took care of most of the men for the past few years, don't forget."

"I can't believe how many GIs have come back this past semester. The campus is swarming with them. The next four years should see larger graduating classes, full of real men!"

"Lucky girls," Beth said as they both left the room, laughing, to join the graduation procession.

On the lawn in front of the chapel, Claudia began to check the crowd going up the steps and waiting at the entrance. She had already given Roger, her fiancé, his ticket, and she had enough left for her two sisters and Mark, plus the extra George had refused. (Nobody was going to catch him sitting through a long "peanut eater" commencement without a smoke!) But where were they, anyway? They had promised to look for her in the lineup and collect their tickets. As she stood apart from the group trying to be conspicuous enough for one of them to spot her, someone came up behind her and touched her arm.

"Oh, hi, Roger. I thought you might be one of the family."

"My reserve-seat privileges give me an extra chance to congratulate the graduate," he said. "Don't forget to meet me right afterward. I have something for you. Mom and Dad are here. They brought something, too."

"How nice! I'm sorry I don't have enough tickets for them. I didn't know they were coming."

"They thought they could only get here in time to pick me and my belongings up afterward. But they made it."

"Well, here's my last one, Roger. Maybe you could let your parents have your own and . . ."

"No, too late. I helped them find quite a good place just back of the reserved section, and they're settled in. Keep the ticket for someone else."

"For me, by chance?" said a deep voice behind them.

"Lucky!"

"Hi there, Claudia. I volunteered to collect the tickets for the Johnsons while they're parking. I'm to meet them at the door and then see if I can squeeze in behind a potted plant somewhere."

"You don't have to do that," Roger said obligingly. "Claudia has another here for . . . her brother, is it?"

Lucky laughed, and Claudia, confused and flustered, stammered, "Roger this is . . . this is Lucky Marshall, an old friend."

The two shook hands. "Now about that ticket for your 'brother,' " Lucky said expectantly, "and the others."

She thrust the four tickets into his hand. "Come on with me," Roger offered, ever friendly. "We'll find Claudia's folks and then get our own seats. Things will begin in less than a half hour, and they'll soon stop holding the reserved ones, so we'd better hurry."

Off they walked together, one tall and dark with a football-player physique, the other thin and blond, and—well, ministerial. What next? she wondered as she tried to gather her wits and find her place in line.

The organ signal soon freed her from her distraction over Lucky's sudden, unexpected arrival, and she fell into the cadence of the processional. At last the high moment arrived as she heard herself summoned forward: "Claudia Jean Foster—With Honors."

"And with 'blood, sweat, toil, and tears,' " she found herself adding mentally on the way to her seat.

Then came the exultant aftermath, a confusion of handclasps, embraces, and tears, of gifts and flowers pressed into her hands, of cameras clicking for pictures posed and unposed. Somewhere in the happy crush, Roger and his parents came and went. She was glad the crowd and distraction of it all had spared her a private goodbye—for a separation she found herself welcoming, and she could only fend off the question she must sooner or later ask herself: Why?

At last the crowd had dwindled. Friends, teachers, other well-wishers had been thanked and promised letters and undying loyalty, and the anticlimax of disposing of academic regalia awaited her. In the press of people milling around, she had lost track of her family since their first quick congratulations and snapshots. But as she headed for the office, the three of them, and Lucky—appearing from behind the library—blocked her path.

"Well, Miss Claudia Foster, B.A., how about a little celebration?" Mark said. "Lucky here suggests a graduation dinner together. What do you say?"

"Oh . . . I don't know . . . should we? I mean, aren't we making a little too much of it?" What she meant but could not say was "Is it socially correct for me to celebrate with Lucky instead of Roger? And why has he turned up again to break my resolution of having nothing more to do with him?" She could see that the others were all for the celebration, however.

"Making too much of it?" Helen was saying. "Not after all your effort."

"And how about that extra citation they read after your

name?" Lucky added. "You need a special time to receive your medals and get your ribbons pinned on!"

When Claudia had finally relented, the five of them crowded into Mark's car and headed toward River Bend. The conversation most of the time centered around the program, the speaker, education in general, and Claudia's new teaching position at Broadvale Academy, in particular. But once during the meal when the others were talking about something else, Lucky was able to initiate a private chat.

"Your Roger is a nice guy, Claudia. And a lucky one, too."

"He'll be a good minister someday."

"But you're going off to teach out of state. No wedding bells yet?"

"Oh, no. Roger has another year of college, and after that it'll be a while before . . ." She found herself postponing the date even beyond their own plans to wait until after Roger's graduation, and again the question arose in her mind—Why?

"Well, I wish you all the best. You know that, don't you?"

"Thanks, Lucky," was all she could say before a question from Gladys brought them back into the conversation.

The meal ended, Lucky and the others left her at her dormitory back at Valley Springs, and drove off. She stood on the steps looking across campus—her *home* for five years. It was all over—graduation, college, a whole long chapter in her life. From now on, she was not only on her own, she was on her own *alone*—facing the world the speaker had so awesomely described. "Well," she told herself emphatically, "you are no longer the student, you are the teacher, so get ready, Miss Foster," and she went in to pack her bags.

* * *

The telephone rang at Bradley's Hardware as Lucky was about to lock up at closing time.

Wouldn't you know, he thought, as he turned the lights on again and went to answer. A dull day from nine to five-thirty, with few customers and fewer phone calls, and now this, just as he was about to leave for home.

"Bradley's," he answered somewhat flatly. "Oh, yes." His voice brightened. "Hello there, Mrs. Johnson. It is? It did? Yes, sure, I'll be right there. I'm just closing up."

After hanging up, he turned off the store lights once again, glanced around to make sure he had everything secured for the night, and locked the door. Climbing into the hardware delivery truck, he headed for the Mark Johnson home.

Mr. Bradley, now getting into his sunset years, left more and more of the responsibility of running the store and the service calls to him. His on-the-job training, sponsored by the GI bill, was paying off, as he regularly took on repair work and installation of appliances.

Now that he had been out of the military for about a year, he was more or less adjusted to civilian life and back into the activities in town. Someone had even put his name up for mayor of Lakeville, but he had quickly withdrawn it. Politics, he knew, was not for him, even if he didn't yet know what exactly was. Having turned 25, he still had time to wait a little for a decision on his future and on marriage. Still, it was time to think of some permanence in his life. Several girls were trying to steer him in that direction, he surmised, so he had been rather careful not to take any of them out more than twice in succession. Keep them guessing, that was his policy these days. But he couldn't help wondering: Was he ready or not to settle down in a place of his own and become a family man?

As he drove across town, the last rays of the evening sun filtered through the tall trees along the street to the Johnsons'. Bright-hued leaves drifted lazily to the ground all around. A great season, fall. He loved the crunch of dried leaves under foot and rake, the smell of smoke permeating the air. Football weather it was, for sure.

But sitting in the stands and rooting for the home team was far different from being in the midst of the action and knowing the cheers were for you. A rhythmic "Lucky, Lucky, Lucky" pulsing through the crowd reached your ears even when you were concentrating your hardest on gaining those yards. Nowadays the players, the cheerleaders, seemed so young. Was he ever that young himself?

He pulled the truck over to the curb and jumped out. Helen Johnson opened the door and led him to her kitchen.

"You see, Lucky?" she said, opening the refrigerator door. "I just defrosted it a few days ago, and now it's melting. The light doesn't go on either."

Lucky was about to open his tool kit when a thought occurred to him. "Just a minute. Let's have a look in back." He stooped down at the side of the refrigerator and peered behind. "I thought this might be the problem," he said, plugging the cord into the outlet. The motor hummed on in quick response.

"Oh, how embarrassing!" Helen said. "I never gave that possibility a thought. In fact, I only noticed the fridge wasn't running when I opened the door to begin supper. I wanted to catch you before the store closed, so I called right away. Guess I should have checked. I'm so sorry for putting you to this unnecessary bother."

"No problem, Mrs. Johnson. I've made a mistake or two myself. I don't blame you for wanting to take care of things at once. I'll just drive the truck back to the store and be on my way home."

"No, wait. I feel so foolish about this, I want to make it up to you. How about staying for supper? Can you? We haven't seen you since Claudia's graduation. Do you mind waiting while I cook?" Helen had already begun pulling things out of the refrigerator and putting them on the deck.

"Well, thanks. I don't have any plans for tonight. I'd be glad to stay. I'll just ring home and tell Mom I won't be coming for supper."

"I hope she won't mind."

Assuring Helen that his mother would not have begun supper yet, he telephoned home, while she hurried about her preparations, scrubbing potatoes, cutting vegetables. She was glad she had half a pie left from yesterday. What a stupid mistake she had made! But anyway, she and Mark would enjoy the company. Lucky was friendly and easy to talk to, and visits from young people like him helped her forget she had no children of her own. Since leaving River Bend, she hadn't had many social outlets. The church in Lakeville had few members, and she had not yet built up an interest in Bible study among her neighbors. It seemed that Lakeville people, entrenched in their small-town habits, were thoroughly churched and extremely loyal to their denominations.

"You know," she said when he had hung up the receiver, "I still can't figure out who unplugged the fridge."

"Maybe your husband wanted to use the outlet," Lucky suggested, "and forgot to plug the cord back in."

"That's possible. I ran over to Gladys' before he left after lunch, so I don't know what he might have done."

"Well, you're back in business now, and as usual, I'm the lucky one. What can I do to help?"

Helen showed him where to find dishes and silverware for setting the table. "That momentary lapse of current reminds me how much we depend on electricity. What did people do without it all those centuries before Franklin and Edison?"

"It is a fairly recent convenience at that."

"When I was a child, Lucky, there were still very few houses outside of town that had it. Can you believe it? And already we're dependent on it everywhere. Well, I believe the Lord had a good reason for reserving some of these modern inventions for the last days."

"Last days, Mrs. Johnson?"

"Yes. Time is running out for our world." Busy stirring a sauce, Helen realized that, while she wanted to lead into spiritual matters, she could not do it and cook at the same time. "But don't let me go into that right now. I can't handle more than one thing—a one-track mind, I'm afraid."

Just then Mark opened the back door, hung his cap and jacket on a hook in the entry, and called, "Helen, I'm home."

As he entered the kitchen his wife greeted him with "Guess who's having supper with us tonight, Mark."

"Well now, let's see. It's hard not to notice a big six-foot-two hardware man putting out the flatware there. Could it possibly be Lucky Marshall?"

"Right on the first guess, hardware, flatware, and all," Lucky said in the same jocular spirit.

Mark shook his hand and slapped him on the back. "Glad to see you."

It wasn't long, while the men waited in the kitchen and talked football, until Helen had supper on the table, and a friendly meal followed. As they finished their dessert, Helen, with significant emphasis toward Mark, announced, "That was the last of the apple pie."

"Too bad. I was about to offer Lucky seconds."

"It's a favorite of mine, folks. I'm just sorry I ate your last piece! But speaking of *last,* before supper you were saying something about last days. Do you believe in the end of the world or something?"

"We—that is, Adventists—have been telling people about it for just about a hundred years now. Soon, we believe, Jesus will come."

"But He already has come—1,946 years ago, right?"

"Yes, that was His first advent. I'm speaking of His second coming."

"I haven't heard much about that, and I've been going to church all my life."

"Not many churches emphasize the fact of Christ's second advent," Helen explained. "Most of them concentrate on the Christmas aspect and forget the promise of the resurrection."

"They seem to think things are going to get better and better in the here and now," Mark added.

"But where are we told that Jesus will come back again? I admit I haven't looked into a Bible since I learned Sunday school memory verses when I was a little kid."

"Let's go in the living room, Lucky. We can find a Bible there."

"How about the dishes? I'm used to helping in the kitchen." Lucky realized he was exaggerating. Usually his mother took care of the washing up. But being with Claudia's sister reminded him of the many times he had helped with the dishes at the Preston home, years ago.

"Not now. We'll let the Martha-work go and be like Mary tonight. Do you know that story, Lucky, the one where Martha asked Jesus to tell Mary to help her with the cooking instead of listening to Him? He quickly pointed out to Martha where her priorities should lie. It's important for us, too, to listen to Him. Besides, if I let you help with the dishes, I'd still 'owe' you for the refrigerator call!"

"What's that?" Mark wanted to know. "What call?"

"Later, dear. Right now Lucky wants to know about the most important event since the resurrection."

\* \* \*

"What I don't understand," Lucky said, "is why, if Jesus really is going to come again, the churches everywhere don't teach it. Why haven't people believed it all along?" He sat on the sofa next to Mark.

"But they *have* believed it. The apostles and the New Testament church certainly did. When they saw Jesus ascending to heaven after His resurrection, they accepted on the spot the promise of His return. Here, you can read about it in the first chapter of Acts. It tells of the last meeting of Jesus with His disciples before His ascension. The verse we are interested in is eleven." Helen handed him a Bible opened to the verse.

" 'Ye men of Galilee,' " Lucky read, " 'why stand ye gazing up into heaven? This same Jesus, which is taken up from you into heaven, shall so come in like manner as ye have seen him go into heaven.' "

"The angel who is speaking here not only promises that Jesus will return but describes the manner of it. The disciples had seen Him slowly ascend into the clouds. Now they are told He will make a very visible return. Read the whole first chapter when you can," Helen suggested.

"The disciples believed that His second coming was so imminent even back then," Mark offered, "that they were very zealous to convert the world to Him."

"You can find an interesting description in 1 Thessalonians where the apostle Paul speaks of the resurrection that takes place at the Second Coming," Helen commented as Lucky turned the unfamiliar pages of the Bible. "Mark can help you find that one. Thanks, Mark."

" 'For the Lord himself shall descend from heaven with a shout,' " Lucky read, " 'with the voice of the archangel, and with the trump of God: and the dead in Christ shall rise first: then we which are alive and remain shall be caught up together with them in the clouds, to meet the Lord in the air: and so shall we ever be with the Lord.' "

"That's a favorite of mine," Mark said.

"It's some text, all right. Reads like Buck Rogers, maybe—'caught up in the clouds' and meeting the Lord 'in the air.' I'm going to show this to my pastor. Let's see, where do I find it? Chapter 4, verses 16 and 17."

"I'm sure your pastor knows it's there, Lucky," Helen said.

"Then why doesn't he preach about it? Christians have certainly lost that zeal you spoke of."

"Yes, they have," Mark agreed. "As time went on and Christianity became the accepted religion of the Western world, the church no longer emphasized the Second Coming."

"I remember studying about Christ in art in my high school art class, and I saw a lot of paintings of the first advent and other events in the life of Jesus, but never any of His coming with angels and trumpets."

"You're right. For centuries when all learning, all art, drama, and architecture resided in the church, when the church was the center of community life, Christianity referred to only one advent—His birth."

"But it revived with the Reformation," Mark added.

"Yes. The Reformers believed in it. Luther, Calvin, and others speak of the Second Coming and the judgment in connection with it."

"It's interesting," Mark said, "that Luther actually tried to predict a time for the judgment. If his prediction had come true, the Lord would have come in the mid-nineteenth century."

"But aren't there always people who want to be prophets and predict doomsday?" Lucky asked.

"That's true. But we must not attempt to go beyond what Scripture has revealed. The Lord Himself never gave us a specific date. He said that no one knows the day or the hour except the Father who is in heaven."

"As the Bible says," Mark continued, "the day of the Lord will come as a thief in the night—that is, unexpectedly. By the way, Lucky, didn't you once tell us of your Scottish ancestry? You might be interested to know that Scotland's Reformer, John Knox, also believed in the Second Coming."

"Knox lived a long time ago, didn't he?" Lucky said. "Like Luther and Calvin. What about more recent well-known preachers?"

"I'm not sure you would know the name William Miller. In the great religious awakening of the nineteenth century, he was widely known for preaching this message and had quite a following. He even set the date for the Advent: 1844."

"He did? What happened to the believers when it didn't take place?"

"I'll have to tell you that whole story someday when you have time. But to answer your question about even more modern times, there is one name you are probably more familiar with—Dwight L. Moody." Helen waited for a sign of recognition from Lucky.

"Oh, yes, I've heard of him."

"Like you, he was in the church a long time—fifteen or sixteen years, he says—before he ever heard of the Second Advent. Then he called it a 'precious doctrine taught in the Bible just as clearly as any other doctrine.' Those are his very words."

"Tell Lucky why Moody thought the doctrine was suppressed."

"I'll just read the rest of the quotation I started a minute ago. I keep it right here in my Bible. Listen to this: 'The devil does not want us to see this truth. . . . The moment a man takes hold of the truth that Jesus Christ is coming back again . . . the world loses its hold on him.'"

I wonder if it could lose its hold on me, Lucky thought as he listened. He also realized that he had not had a cigarette since he left the store at five-thirty. Eating supper and later concentrating on the discussion had helped him disregard the urge to light up. But now the desire was upon him so strongly he knew he had to leave, or ask permission to smoke.

Aloud he said, "I certainly have a lot to learn." He fidgeted in his shirt pocket for his pack and then stopped himself. "Don't some churches teach that Christ is already here? Seems I've heard that someplace."

"They do. But if He is here, then Scripture is false. Because the Bible tells how He will come, as you read in 1 Thessalonians."

"And in Matthew," Mark said. "Here, let me read you Matthew 24:23: 'Then if any man shall say unto you, Lo, here is Christ, or there; believe it not.' Then verse 27: 'For as the lightning cometh out of the east, and shineth even unto the west; so shall also the coming of the Son of man be.'"

Helen sensed Lucky's restlessness at this point and knew they must end their discussion. "You know how the Bible ends, Lucky?" she asked. The last book concludes with 'Even so, come, Lord Jesus.' Those of us who love Him want Him to come. We want to be in His kingdom."

"Well, this is all pretty new to me, Mr. and Mrs. Johnson," Lucky said, rising. "It interests me very much. In fact, I'm going to read the Bible. Where shall I start?"

"The Gospels, I'd say. Wouldn't you, Helen?"

"Yes. A person reading the Bible for the first time does well to start in the New Testament."

"My church apparently doesn't believe in the Old Testament. Apart from Psalms and Proverbs, it is never mentioned."

"The story of Christ is just as much a theme of the Old

Testament as of the New, of course," Helen commented.

"It is? Would you mind if I came again and talked to you about it? I think I'd like a little guidance from someone who knows more than I do."

"You're certainly welcome, Lucky. Why not come next Sunday?" Mark suggested. "We're free then, aren't we, Helen?"

His wife nodded her ready assent.

"A great idea," Lucky observed, "studying the Bible on the Lord's Day. I'll be here about three, if that's all right. I have to leave now. Thanks for a good supper."

"And thanks for coming, Lucky."

After they saw him out the door, Helen could hardly wait to express her pleasure at the turn of events. "Mark," she said, "did you pull the plug on the refrigerator at noon? Because if you didn't, an angel must have!"

* * *

Mrs. Johnson awaited Lucky's coming the following Sunday with inner trepidation. She hoped Mark would leave his puttering in the basement and join her soon because she needed his moral support as well as his silent prayers. Helen felt totally inadequate to discuss the subject she had chosen. To awaken Lucky's awareness of his need of a Saviour, to present to him the sublime themes of the plan of salvation—it was too much for a mere high school graduate like herself, untutored in theology. But the Lord had not failed her yet. He had led people to Himself through her in River Bend. Here was another for her to direct to truth. Her feeble human efforts, combined with His strength, could work the miracle. *If* he remembered to come. Already it was nearly three-thirty.

The doorbell rang. When she opened the door, Lucky stood expectantly on the steps.

"You won't believe how hard it was for me to get here," he said. "First, my mother tried to get me to stay and see friends of hers and Dad's, then just as I was leaving, a longtime friend of mine showed up at the door. Wanted me to go bowling."

"How did you resist that?" Mark asked, joining them in the living room.

"I told him, 'Sorry, pal, right now I have an important engagement.' "

"I hope you don't feel cheated, giving up some fun with your friend," Helen said, the challenge of proving more interesting than a bowling match now facing her.

"Not at all. I can bowl any day, especially any day but Sunday. We've always avoided sports and such on Sunday at our house."

"We feel the same in keeping Sabbath," Mark said.

"That's Saturday for you, isn't it?"

"And—ever since Eden—for all mankind," Helen couldn't resist saying. Then to avoid going into a topic she hoped to continue at a later date, she said quickly, "Today I thought we would talk a little about the great controversy."

"Great controversy. This is something in the Bible?"

"Yes. Not called by that name in the concordances, of course. It's a controversy or struggle that's been going on since before Creation."

*"Before* Creation! When in the world was that? I thought you couldn't go further back than the beginning. That's what I read about in Genesis this past week, by the way. Decided to start in both the Old and the New Testament. Didn't get much past 'In the beginning,' though. Too many *begats!"*

"Keep going anyway, Lucky," Mark urged. "You'll get used to those. In fact, try a more modern version, one a little easier than the King James. But back to the great controversy."

"Lucky, you're a soldier," Helen began. "It might interest you to know about the war in heaven."

"War in *heaven?* Wait a minute! Don't tell me that's in the Bible."

"Yes, it's all a part of the great controversy."

"Between who? Between *whom,* I think I'd say if Miss Beardsley, my English teacher, were here listening in."

"Between two opposing angelic forces led by Michael

and Lucifer."

"In my high school days—speaking of Miss Beardsley— we were always studying the conflict between good and evil in the different classics. But I never heard of one between Michael and Lucifer."

"Well, in this war, Michael—the name for Christ in His preexistence—led the forces who remained loyal to God; and Lucifer, who was to become Satan, headed the rebelling forces. They were trying to topple the government of God, Lucky. Lucifer lost and God had to cast him out of heaven with one third of the angels who had lined up with him."

"You mean they fought with actual arms—swords or guns or something?"

"We really can't say what kind of combat it was. The Bible, you know, is written in human terms. We only know it was a real struggle, the beginning of this great controversy I've been speaking of, between Christ and Satan. You can find an account of it in Revelation, chapter 12."

"That's the last book, isn't it?" Lucky took the Bible she handed him and read the place indicated: "'And there was war in heaven: Michael and his angels fought against the dragon; and the dragon fought and his angels, and prevailed not; . . . and the great dragon was cast out, that old serpent, called the Devil, and Satan, which deceiveth the whole word; he was cast out into the earth, and his angels were cast out with him'" (verses 7-9).

Lucky stopped reading. He looked pensive. "There's no arguing about the fact there was a war. But my pastor once said that the book of Revelation is a mystery, totally symbolic. Can we take this literally?"

"However we interpret the way the war was fought," Helen answered, "there's hardly any way to symbolize away the struggle. It was real."

"Well, if Satan and his angels were deported, didn't that end the conflict? Why didn't the Lord just destroy them and end evil right on the spot? And why did He exile them to earth to bring their mischief here?"

"Those are questions men have been asking through the

ages, Lucky," Mark said.

"But they do have answers," Helen assured him. "You just finished reading verse 9 of chapter 12. In the next verse see what Satan is called besides devil and dragon."

Lucky found his place in the Bible again and scanned down the page. "I see he's called the 'accuser of our brethren.'"

"Right. Well, he is also the accuser of God. The Bible tells us that he—a created being—wanted to be like the Creator."

"Isaiah 14 tells about the jealousy that arose in his heart and about his lofty ambitions to be like the Most High—the Lord Himself. But he was a created being." Mark leafed through his Bible. "And here in Ezekiel 28 there's another picture of him. He was a covering cherub, we are told. It says he was perfect in all his ways till iniquity was found in him."

"But if he was *perfect*," Lucky wanted to know, "how could it be?"

"That is one of two great mysteries Paul speaks of in his writings," Helen explained. "We can never solve them this side of eternity—the mystery of godliness and the mystery of iniquity. Why not read those chapters in Isaiah and Ezekiel at home when you have time. They tell about the spirit of envy that drove Lucifer to launch a campaign among the angels to discredit God."

"If God had destroyed him, the doubts he had planted in the unfallen beings in the universe would have been unanswered," Mark said, "and they would have served Him from fear—fear of also being destroyed—rather than from love."

"That seems logical," Lucky replied, deep in thought.

"God values nothing more than the freedom of His children. He has given us all—every created being in the universe—the freedom of choice," Mark went on.

"So the answer to your question as to why Satan's hosts were exiled in earth," Helen continued, "is that God quarantined them here where He is allowing the great controversy to be played out. It is here that sin is to have its full reign, to prove to the universe the ultimate results of rebellion against God and separation from Him.

"Just think, Lucky, this earth is the theater where the drama of the ages is being staged—and every human being ever born is an actor in it. Each of us has a chance to accept the truth about God, or accept Satan's lies about Him."

"Couldn't God have kept Satan from tempting Adam and Eve?"

"Yes, certainly, but again, that would have been forced obedience. Instead of being free moral agents, they would have been mere automatons. God doesn't want to be served by robots, but by those who love and trust Him—who understand to what lengths He went to prove His love, by giving His Son to win back dominion of the earth from Satan."

"Sometime soon," Mark suggested, "you must read the story of Job. It is a summary, actually, of the way the great controversy goes on. God permitted Satan to cause successive calamities—the death of Job's children, the loss of his property—to fall on him, to prove to the heavenly councils, where the 'accuser of our brethren' was at work, that Job would still be faithful. Job didn't know, of course, that it was a test."

"So it was Satan who caused all the troubles," said Helen. "Job's wife and his friends thought his troubles were punishments from God for sins committed."

"It's always Satan who causes men's troubles, Lucky," Mark said.

"Mark is right. Satan attacks us where we are weakest. And God allows us to be tested as Job was, to prove that we are safe to save in His kingdom. But He turns those tests to our good, as Romans 8:28 tells us, and to the vindication of God. Satan's evil ways are thus exposed."

"What about Adam and Eve? They must have been a big disappointment to God."

"Before they ever sinned, Lucky," Helen told him, "God had provided that one of the Trinity would accept the ultimate consequence of sin, which is final death, final separation from Him."

"You know that's really never been clear to me, though I have been celebrating Easter all my life. Why did Jesus have to die?"

"Satan accused God of being arbitrary and unfair," Helen explained. "Jesus' death left no doubt that He is more than fair, not willing that any but Himself should suffer the penalty of disobedience. When Jesus willingly gave up His exalted position in heaven that Satan was so jealous of and came here to die in place of man, it put all doubts about the love and justice of God to rest."

" 'God so loved the world, that he gave his only begotten Son.' You know that verse, don't you?" Mark asked.

"Sure thing. Learned it when I was a kindergartner. But I never understood before what it meant."

"What thrills me," Helen said, "is that God the Father gave His Son forever to the human race. Now that Jesus has returned to His Father, He will forever retain His human form and be our representative in the councils of heaven. He has deposed the usurper."

"That's something I never realized. It's tremendous."

"And furthermore, He would have done it for you or me or Mark, had one of us been the only rebellious creature in the universe. He loves us that much, Lucky."

A wave of gratitude engulfed Lucky. "Now I know why He saved my life on the battlefield. To save me in His kingdom."

"In the great controversy that is still going on, Satan is battling Christ for your heart and mine," Helen explained. "When we choose Satan's side, we crucify Jesus anew."

"Well, I certainly want to be on God's side," Lucky responded with conviction. "I'd feel like a traitor, joining the enemy ranks."

"Good for you, Lucky!" Mark said.

"Once you line up with God in the great controversy, He begins to prepare you for citizenship in His kingdom," Helen added.

"When can I learn more about that, Mr. and Mrs. Johnson?"

"Why not come back next Sunday?" Mark suggested.

"You know, I have evenings free after work."

"Choose any evening you want, Lucky," Helen replied sensing his urgency.

"May I come tomorrow night?"

So it was settled that they would have another study the next night, and Lucky left whistling.

When they had closed the door after him, Mark commented, "The Lord helped you take the right approach, Helen."

"I only scratched the surface, of course, and I said very little about being saved by grace, through faith in Jesus. But there's time for that as we go along."

"Lucky is a likable fellow, isn't he?"

"If only he had shown this interest before Claudia settled her future with Roger," Helen replied.

\* \* \*

The question was what to do about Roger. Claudia's red pen poised in a hand holding the chin of a most perplexed countenance. A sheaf of tenth-grade compositions lay before her untouched. Ticking away precious evening minutes, the clock on the desk in her room at Broadvale Academy reminded her insistently of her neglected duties.

For three months now she had been leading the busy, interesting, sometimes hectic life of a teacher. So far, she had things quite well in control. Her students in French were upperclassmen, most of them serious and mature, all of them likable.

The challenge in her ninth-grade English class was to keep the boys awake at one in the afternoon after their full morning of work—especially the dairy boys. Poor fellows, they had to get up at 3:00 A.M. to milk. Often she didn't have the heart to wake them up when they dozed off. It seemed to her their sleep was more important than knowing the difference between an adjective clause and an adverb one. Heresy for an English teacher, she mused, pure heresy! Fortunately, you couldn't be condemned to the stake for your thoughts.

## IN RETROSPECT: THE WAY IT ALL HAPPENED

As for the sophomore English class, she had to admit it was the one heavy burden of her class load, taxing every ounce of patience and resourcefulness she possessed. Twenty-two boys and three girls, not one of them caring a comma for grammar or poetry or writing. No wonder the administration had assigned them to the slow section, and the slow section to the most junior member of the staff.

It was they, she was sure, who had turned off the lights in the study hall on her night to supervise this past week and let the bat loose in the room. She had succeeded in stemming the tide of squealing girls toward the door, getting them back in their seats and the smirking boys once more at their books. Keeping one eye peeled on the bat hanging on one of the light fixtures, she had lasted out the evening and passed the test—with flying colors, the principal had said.

It was therefore not teaching problems that preoccupied her at nine-thirty that cold November evening. It was Roger. Ever since she had arrived at Broadvale—away from the familiar surroundings of Valley Springs, where she used to walk the campus paths with him—she had increasingly stronger misgivings about her feelings toward him. At the same time, living in the home of his aunt and uncle, she felt inextricably bound to his future, committed to keeping her promise to him.

With continued detachment, she stretched the silver band on the engagement watch Roger had given her and let it snap back. She knew that Elder and Mrs. Landers had only agreed to take her into their home because of their nephew. Yet when he came for a weekend visit last month, and had talked of being offered a pastorate, she had been decidedly uncomfortable about the plans he tried to discuss, involving where they would live. Again she had found herself postponing the wedding date.

"You have to face up to it, Claudia Foster," she told herself, rising abruptly. "You don't want to marry Roger Landers. Admit it."

"Yes, but even if you got up the courage to tell him so, you'd have to face up to one fact," she argued with herself.

"Which is, that you would no doubt be signing up for spinsterhood. How many single men are going to come into your life at isolated Broadvale?"

Reluctantly she let the inevitability of spinsterhood lodge in her consciousness as she paced the room.

"So I'd rather be single than married to the wrong person."

There! She had said it aloud. Things were out in the open. No longer did she need to pretend anything to herself. She seized the first paper on the pile and vigorously applied the red pen. Now, she thought, I can get down to business. And she did.

\* \* \*

"Hi, Miss Foster." It was one of her brightest senior girls.

"Hello, Gerry. Going my way?"

"If I can walk you home."

"You surely may. Only for exercise, or are you needing help?"

"Both. Here, let me carry something for you. My, it looks as if you have more homework than I do." The two fell into step, walking off campus on a lane dusted with the first snow of the winter.

"There are always papers and plans and grades after teaching hours. I guess I knew it would be this way. I'm glad Christmas vacation is coming, aren't you?"

"I thought only kids felt that way."

"Well, now you know. Still want to be a teacher?"

"Oh, yes. French, maybe English."

"Is that what you want my help for—deciding what to teach?" Claudia suspected the choice of a teaching emphasis was far from what the girl was thinking of, but she wanted to give her a lead. Often, she had learned, the young boarding students needed to talk and were shy about initiating a conversation.

"Well, no, not exactly. Miss Foster . . . how does it feel to be in love?"

Trying not to appear as taken aback as she was, Claudia answered, "The way you feel at 16 is usually quite different from the way you feel at 25."

Twenty-five! Claudia's own mother had married at 18. At 25 a single woman in that long-ago day was a confirmed old maid. But inside, she herself felt no older than this 16-year-old, in spite of what she had just told her. Would it always be that way? she wondered. Certainly she felt no wiser at 25, least of all in matters of love. So far she had not scored very high, two broken engagements behind her and one pending.

"It's Johnny, Miss Foster."

Claudia jerked herself back to reality. What had Gerry been telling her while her mind drifted to her own concerns?

"Johnny Myers, I take it. I've noticed you two together around campus lately."

"Yes. He's really keen, don't you think?"

"Well, he's not bad, I'll agree." All arms and legs and braces, she thought to herself. "What is your problem with Johnny?"

"Oh, it's no *problem.* I just wonder if he's the one for me."

"Depends on what you mean by that. If you mean the one to take you to the Christmas banquet, I'd say Yes, I'm sure he's the one. But if you mean he's forever, I'm afraid I can't answer that, Gerry. Some academy couples eventually marry. Most do not. But no one else can tell you if he's 'the one.'"

"But how do you know when a person *is* the right one?"

How indeed! Claudia thought.

"How did you know Elder Landers' nephew was the one for you, Miss Foster," the girl persisted. "I saw him when he was here a while back. He's cute!"

"Here we are already, Gerry," Claudia said, glad that the afterthought about Roger's "cuteness" had spared her answering the question. "Thanks for carrying my things and for your company. Can you come in?"

"No, I've got to get to the cafeteria. I might land at Johnny's table if I hurry."

"I'd say you've got things pretty well figured out! But my

advice to you, Gerry, is to start praying now that you'll recognize 'the one' when he comes along."

"Thanks, Miss Foster. See you in class tomorrow." She handed Claudia her bag and ran off to meet her boyfriend.

Going to her room, Claudia dumped her things on her desk, wishing life were so simple for her. In the weeks since she had decided Roger was not 'the one' for her, she'd wrestled with the problem of how to tell the Landerses. And Roger, of course. But Elder and Mrs. Landers, close at hand, were her first hurdle. She had followed her advice to Gerry—she had prayed that the Lord would impress her with the right decision. Not wanting to hurt him, she had prayed that if Roger was the one after all, her feelings would change accordingly.

Elder Landers' study door opened and he went into the living room to read the evening paper, as was his custom. Mrs. Landers was giving their 2-year-old son his evening bath. It was a propitious moment to face the pastor and seek his counsel. Breathing a quick prayer, she joined him, sitting down on the footstool at his feet.

"Have you a minute to talk?"

He looked up from his newspaper. "Sure, Claudia. What is it? Sophomore headaches or senior sponsorship decisions?"

"Nothing like that. I . . . I just want to know—well, to get directly to the point—would you think any less of me if I broke my engagement to Roger?"

The man's bushy blond brows arched abruptly. He laid his newspaper aside and leaned forward in his chair. "You don't love him, Claudia?"

He seemed so formidable, this tall, granite-featured man with the craggy brow and the ice-blue eyes. Suddenly she felt weak and shaky, but no less certain of what she should say. "No, I don't, Elder Landers."

"Then I would think far less of you if you went ahead and married him," he said simply.

"I can't tell you how relieved that makes me feel. I've been so worried how you would take it."

"Claudia, don't ever let what others think deter you from making a decision you feel—with God's help—to be the right one."

The blue eyes focused on her were not really that icy. They reflected the understanding and sympathy this man of God felt for her.

"Thanks, Pastor, I'll try to remember that. Because I still have to face Roger."

"It'll be hard, Claudia, but it's best you do this now rather than live to regret it. I know Roger's folks wouldn't want you to suppress your feelings just to spare him pain. They'll be sorry—they like you very much. He'll be hurt, but the Lord will see everyone through the ordeal."

"Don't let on to anyone here before I tell Roger, please. I'll not even say anything to my sisters yet. I won't be seeing them, anyway, this Christmas. Instead I'm going to spend the holidays right here."

"You don't want to be with your relatives?"

"Well, yes, but I'm not very accustomed to taking vacations. And besides, I have loads of things to do here, and I want to be more ready for second semester than I was for first—now that I know my program and my students."

"Roger isn't expecting you to spend Christmas with him?"

"He's going West with his mother and dad. He wasn't planning to, but I insisted."

"I see why now."

"Yes, I'm afraid it was a dodging maneuver. I'll wait to tell him about us when he gets back and finishes his first-semester exams—so that he won't be too upset to do well."

"A good idea. But don't wait long after that. No use to postpone the inevitable."

"I hope you won't mind my staying here over the holidays."

"Not at all. You're one of the family already. Little Eddy just adores you. And Lillian hasn't yet finished her fattening-up process on you. She says you still need to gain ten pounds. The holidays are an excellent time for that."

"Her cooking any time guarantees fattening up!" Claudia said, feeling unusually lighthearted and relieved.

"One of the family." She remembered those words as she returned to her room. They had a nice ring to them, she decided.

\* \* \*

One of Claudia's Christmas cards was from Elaine Paulsen, in whose home she had met the man who had been influential in getting her to Valley Springs years before. Now as principal of Broadvale, Mr. Hanson had also given her her first teaching post. His cousin, Mrs. Paulsen, had kept in close touch with her through the years.

The Christmas card contained a check. "With this," Mrs. Paulsen wrote, "I want you to come for a weekend in River Bend soon. We haven't seen much of you since the summer you stayed with us, and we're lonesome for you. You're the closest we've come to having a daughter."

Claudia reflected on the words of Scripture Helen had quoted to her the day their father had taken his stand against her joining the Adventist Church, the verse about forsaking father and mother for His sake. Certainly within the church, she had acquired a larger family than ever. More than one had told her she was part of the family, that she was like a daughter. It was very comforting. The Paulsens had even hired her as a companion-"housegirl" one summer during college—which had helpd her budget considerably.

With the fare to River Bend provided, Claudia could hardly refuse. Besides, she needed to get away briefly. All work and no play was no healthier for her than for dull-boy Jack. She had accomplished a number of things on her vacation list. It was time to take a break.

Just as she sat sat down to write Mrs. Paulsen that she would be there the following weekend—her last before school resumed—Mrs. Landers knocked on her door.

"Telephone for you, Claudia."

"Who is it, do you know?" Fervently she hoped that it

wasn't Roger. It was difficult keeping him at arm's length without arousing suspicion.

"I don't think so, but it *is* a man's voice."

Mystified, she heard the voice say, "Hello, Claudia, how are you?"

"Quite well, thank you," she answered, puzzling over its familiar sound. Then suddenly she knew. "Why, Phil! Phil Gardner! Where are you?"

"I'm in River Bend with my brother and his family. My first trip east since I left for med school more than three years ago."

"What a surprise, Phil."

She could not think of what else to say. Memories flooded her mind. Phil had been one of the few eligible men on the college campus during the lean war years and had totally captured her heart. The fact that they both had River Bend relatives, strangely enough, had not been the occasion of their meeting and later falling deeply in love.

Before the war started, she had gone to the lyceum programs—the only option open for a date—with various young men, only one or two of whom had interested her beyond the evening's program. Somehow during her first years in school the tall image of Lucky still intruded on those occasions, and her partner always emerged from the inevitable comparison as the unlucky one.

Then when Pearl Harbor thinned the ranks of eligibles at rapid rates, she felt particularly fortunate to be noticed by the one young man she realized could replace Lucky very handily. He was intelligent, he was good-looking and witty, and he was a Seventh-day Adventist. As a premed, he was also exempt from the draft. For more than a year she had enjoyed the pleasure of his company. On a Christmas night he had asked her to wait for him to finish medical school, and she promised she would.

"Are you still there, Claudia?"

"Yes, Phil. I was wondering how long you'll be in River Bend."

"A couple of weeks. I wish I could see you."

Claudia remembered that she would be in River Bend herself in a few days. Should she tell him so? "I'm going to visit the Paulsens this weekend, Phil," she heard herself say.

"You are? Great! It was Mrs. Paulsen I called to find out where you were." Was this a conspiracy? Claudia wondered. Surely not. Mrs. Paulsen didn't know yet of her plan to break her engagement to Roger. "She didn't tell me you were coming," Phil continued. "I wonder why."

No conspiracy, just coincidence. "That's because she didn't know. I was just now beginning a letter to her about it."

"Will you save Saturday night for me?"

"Why yes, if it will be all right with the Paulsens."

"I'll work on that angle before you get here. See you then."

Trying to analyze her feelings, Claudia hung up the telephone. Was this a new development in her life, more than just a coincidence that she would be in River Bend when Phil was there? Hadn't she settled it already that he was no more *"the* one" for her than Roger? Their relationship had not been strong enough to stand the tests of time and distance.

Phil had not made her feel needed, vital to his happiness. His casual way of relegating her to secondary importance, below his medical priorities, made her feel like an adjunct in his plans instead of the one about whom she felt they should revolve. He had let her drift out of his life so easily. No passionate pleas of I love you, I need you, had followed her suggestion that perhaps they should free each other of promises made. They had never announced those promises to anyone but her roommate anyway. Claudia had wanted to shout their engagement from the rooftops, but Phil seemed to want to keep it quiet for a while. Med school, that was paramount. As it had to be, she realized. Still, she had been hurt.

It was that hurt, she knew now, that had made her ripe for a rebound romance. And along had come Roger.

My young friend Gerry thinks I have all the answers, she

mused. Well, I'm the last to advise in matters of love. It's too complicated for me. Better, perhaps, to be an old maid after all!

\* \* \*

Elaine Paulsen was setting the table when Claudia entered the room.

"Claudia, you look stunning," said the older woman. "Phil is going to be simply dazzled."

"I'm not sure I want to dazzle him, Mrs. Paulsen. In fact, I'm not even sure at this point I should see him. But he's coming any minute now, so I can't change my mind. It was nice of you to invite him for supper, anyway."

"Only to have your company tonight. He was very determined to steal you away this evening, and very persuasive. Better be alert to those powers of persuasion!"

"I doubt he could have persuaded you of anything unless you were willing. I think you rather like him."

"I do, Claudia. He's been in our River Bend church since he was a cute little youngster. It will be a double treat to have you both with us tonight. Now that you've told me about Roger, I can't help hoping you two will get together again."

At that moment the doorbell rang. "Shall I go?" Claudia asked, her heart suddenly turning a cartwheel. When she opened the door, three years of her life faded away. Here was the same tall, slim young man with the electric blue eyes, grinning at her as if he had just got permission for a parlor date from the dean back in the dorm.

She extended her hand and he took both hers in his. "Hello, Duchess."

Her heart turned another cartwheel. He hadn't forgotten his pet name for her. Only when very serious did he call her Claudia.

"Hello, Phil. Come on in," she said somewhat tremulously.

"Yes, come in, Phil. It's good to see you after so long," Mrs. Paulsen added shaking his hand. "I'll take your coat."

"Thanks again for the invitation, Mrs. Paulsen. I couldn't possibly afford to take Claudia out to eat. Not with med school costing what it does and that appetite of hers."

"Always joking, aren't you, Phil?" He had a way of combining the factual with the ridiculous so humorously that she never could top him. "You know I eat like a bird."

"That's what I mean. Have you ever watched a bird *eat?*"

"Enough of this talk. I'm beginning to wonder if I've prepared enough food! We'll call Henry now and come to table."

The meal that followed was leisurely and pleasant. Phil kept them entertained with tales of school and travel experiences in what he called the "western frontier." When it was over, Claudia offered to clear the dishes off the table. As she put them in the kitchen sink she heard Phil telling the Paulsens, "I'll bring her back before midnight, I promise."

"Back from where, Phil?" she asked, rejoining the three in the dining room. "Isn't it too cold and snowy to venture out?"

"It's a beautiful night, clear and frosty, the kind I don't want to waste.When I'm drowning in sunshine back at school, I'll need some cool reserves stored up," he answered. "And you need to walk off some of those calories you just stowed away."

Claudia laughed. Phil must have noticed how little she actually ate. Her fragile appetite never held up under any kind of tension or excitement, a fact Mrs. Landers couldn't seem to understand as she added dollops of whipped cream to Claudia's portions of her famous pies. Eating at Mrs. Landers' home had become a serious undertaking, and she was glad to get away with virtually nothing on her plate here at the Paulsens.

"Did *you* walk here, Phil?" she challenged.

"No. To tell you the truth, I want you to have a ride in my brand-new secondhand chariot. My first car."

They drove to Main Street and parked in the municipal parking lot. "Come on, Duchess, let's look at the shop windows, the way we used to."

It surprised Claudia at how many of their previous activities Phil remembered. As struggling college students, they had little to spend on entertainment. The Saturday night programs—with ten minutes allowed afterward by strictly chaperoning deans—usually provided their recreation. But sometimes when they visited their respective relatives in River Bend, they had a Saturday night—in Phil's words—"on the town." It meant walking hand in hand along Main Street, window-shopping, picking out furnishings for a home envisioned years in the future.

Now here they were again, hand in hand, walking the same avenue, window-shopping. Somehow the crisp January air failed to penetrate the warmth of their enjoyment. They priced and "purchased," rejected and "returned" item after item of clothing, furniture, silver, china. Then it began to snow light flakes that sparkled on Phil's black hair and clung to Claudia's lashes.

"I'd better get you inside, Duchess, before you freeze. You've spent far too much tonight, anyway. I always knew I couldn't afford you."

"It's only my tastes that are expensive, Phil."

As she joked she thought how hard she found stretching her modest salary to cover her living expenses, replenishing a long-deficient wardrobe, and repaying a small loan for her last year of school.

She climbed into the car as Phil held the door for her. Instead of brushing away the fast accumulating snow on the windshield, Phil got in beside her. "Before it gets too cold to sit here, Claudia, let's talk awhile. It's not midnight yet, is it?"

Pulling up her sleeve, she held her arm toward the street light outside and tried to see the time. It occurred to her that she was still wearing Roger's watch. Though she no longer considered herself engaged, was she wrong to be in Phil's company? First Lucky, now Phil. Why must the past come back to disturb her like this?

Phil took her arm and looked at the time. "A nice watch you have there, Claudia."

Not Duchess this time. She knew he was serious. No doubt wondering about the watch. Now she wished she hadn't worn it. They sat silently in the white cocoon of the car. Then Phil broke the silence.

"You know something, Claudia? No one else has ever taken your place with me."

Cartwheels again! What could she say? She knew it was an opening she wanted to seize, to say, "I'm glad, Phil. I hope no one ever will." Why, just those few words would do it. Goodbye spinsterhood!

But the words froze on her lips. She shivered.

"You're cold. I'll take you back to the Paulsens'." He got out and brushed the snowy fluff off the windshield and side windows, turned on the motor, and they drove away. They said little until they arrived at the door. Taking her hands, Phil asked, "When will I see you again, Claudia?"

In her mind she answered, why not take me to the train tomorrow—or all the way to Broadvale—and after that . . . Instead, she found herself saying, "Maybe . . . Phil . . . in three more years . . ."

"Good night, Claudia. Thanks for a nice evening."

Turning on his heel, he strode to the car.

She stood motionless, willing herself to call after him, to invite him back. But her mouth refused to open, her lips to move. It was as if a cold hand covered her mouth, smothering her words. Then hurrying into the house and into her room, she flung herself on the bed, and cried hot, silent tears.

* * *

Claudia looked up from a desk littered with papers. Mrs. Landers stood at the door in her dressing gown. "It's very late, my dear. Aren't you about finished? Your eyes are as red as your marking pen."

"I've just about got my grades done at last. I must say it hurts teachers worse than it does students, giving tests. First, making them up, then marking them, then adding and averaging points. What a job!"

"I know. I've been through many years of this with Will. He always wrestles so with each student's grade."

"It's the worst part of teaching, I've learned. Trying to be both accurate and objective. But what are you doing up at this hour?"

"I was checking on Eddy and saw your light. I'm concerned about the sleep you're losing, working so hard."

"I'm used to it from college. I'll do better tomorrow night."

"Well, I hope so. Good night, Claudia."

"Good night, Mrs. Landers. Thanks for your concern." After all her years almost on her own, it was rather nice, Claudia realized, to be mothered again, even at age 25.

A half hour later she entered her last grade and put down her pen. As she gathered up the papers and packed her briefcase for the next day, she breathed a sigh of relief. Her first semester of teaching was behind her. But it was also end-of-semester at Valley Springs, she reminded herself at once. Roger would be done with his tests this week. Now was the time to face up to their situation. But how to tell him, how least to hurt him? All the while she got ready for bed, the questions tortured her.

It occurred to her then that she had postponed breaking the engagement as much to avoid the ordeal as to spare Roger the distraction from his studies. While consumed with exams and grades, she could keep the matter at bay. Now, however, there was no further reprieve—she must do what she had to do. But how could she!

"Oh, dear God," she prayed, "help me through this hard time."

As she lay trying to go to sleep she heard the mantel clock chime one o'clock, then two. Roger . . . Phil . . . Lucky . . . She had been with all three at different times in the past six months, and the emotional turmoil involved had far outweighed any pleasure she had had. She thought of Miss Winters, the librarian at Broadvale. Unmarried, in her 40s, jovial and good-natured. Small wonder! Her life was her own. No complicated matters of heart to deal with. Yes, it was time to take a leaf from the librarian's book.

But first she must take care of the Roger problem. As her mind raced on, she grew desperate—she had to relax and get some sleep! At last she realized her only solution, the one she had turned to all during school days. Slipping out of the covers, she knelt by her bed.

"Lord, I am a coward. I can't face Roger, I can't face his folks. Please impress him to break our engagement. Please, please, make *him* do it, not me."

Then she fell asleep.

Late one afternoon early in February Pastor Landers stopped by her classroom where she was still busy putting a valentine motif on the bulletin board. He stood looking at her display, tentatively pronouncing the French words on the placards: *amour, fiancé, mariage.*

"The kids shouldn't have any difficulty concentrating on this vocabulary, Claudia."

"We try to make it as painless as possible," she said, smiling, "though they'll soon learn that love is not a valentine. It can be even more painful than learning French."

"I take it you're speaking from personal experience. Still haven't faced up to things with Roger, Claudia?"

"No, but soon. I've been praying."

"Well, I just came back to school to get my grade book—I've finished another set of papers—and I thought I'd drop off your mail." He handed her a large envelope. "I see it's from Roger."

"Thanks, Pastor." As he walked off down the hall, she stood looking at Roger's familiar writing, not wanting to open the envelope. When she finally did, she saw it was a large valentine card, all hearts and flowers, addressed to "Darling."

She winced. How unkind of her to keep him in the dark since before Christmas, to let him go on planning their future. Condemned, she determined to write him that very night. She opened the card, read the message of loving devotion, and turned to the note on the back.

"I've been strongly impressed the past few days, Claudia, that it's all over between us. If you say that's not true, I'll be in seventh heaven. If it is true, you know I'll be crushed. But I won't hold you to your promises—the engagement, I'm afraid, is off . . ."

For a long moment she let waves of relief and reverence wash over her. An understanding heavenly Father had once again answered her prayers.

"Thank You, Lord," she breathed. "Oh, thank You." Then down the hall she raced, fairly singing, "Pastor Landers, guess what!"

\* \* \*

The rest of the days dropped off the February calendar like ripe fruit. Claudia, relieved of an enormous burden, felt the first glimmers of spring in her soul, in spite of lingering snow and ice. Her zest for life picked up, her satisfaction in her work took on new dimensions. She had written Roger and explained the doubts and misgivings that had led to her decision, and she had returned the watch. Now she was single and free and dedicated to the Lord's service. Without any concern that spinsterhood threatened her, that she had within weeks sent her last two prospects for marriage out of her life, she felt quite prepared to enjoy living as much as Miss Winters seemed to. Why, it was possible now, once she had caught up with herself financially, to go right on to a Master's degree, maybe even a Ph.D. What a heady thought!

One March day a letter arrived from Helen.

"The last couple of months I've been having a most gratifying series of Bible studies," she wrote. "You'll never guess with whom. *Lucky!* Can you believe it? So far he is keenly interested in everything I've presented.

"At first we dealt mostly with the love of God. I've explained to him that it isn't anything we do, or don't do, that saves us; it is what Jesus has done for us. His death was ours, our life is covered by His righteousness. Our only part is to surrender to Him.

"You know, he has had the same impression so many have, that Adventists believe they are saved by keeping the law. No such thing, I told him. Even the very best we can offer in obedience comes nowhere near keeping the *spirit* of the law, even *if* we could perfectly observe the *letter*.

"Lucky has been genuinely touched. Pray for him. Love,

Helen."

Claudia folded the letter thoughtfully and put it back in the envelope. Could it *possibly* be that one day he would actually become an Adventist, that she . . . that they . . . that this was why she had been held back in spite of herself from encouraging Phil that January night?

But no! She was not going to count on anything. After all, she herself had had some hopeful moments with him in Lakeville at Christmastime, only to have her hopes dashed. Reminding herself of that distant doctorate, she decided to keep from getting involved—but of course she would pray.

The next day as she walked to her room where she met her prayer band after chapel on Wednesday mornings, her faithful friend Gerry overtook her.

"Hi, Miss Foster. You know what? Johnny and I broke up last night. But I don't care, really I don't. I like Glenn; he's more dependable."

"And he does his homework, besides," Claudia said. "As if that matters to you as much as to me."

"Can I ask you a personal question, Miss Foster? We—that is, some of us—have noticed you're not wearing your watch these days. Aren't you engaged to Elder Landers' nephew anymore? We hope so. He's swell."

"You girls don't miss anything, do you? Well, you're right; he is, and we're not. Do you think I'll make a proper old maid?"

"Never!"

"Come on, Gerry. We've got to hurry. It's time for prayer band. I have a special request to present. I'm praying for a man . . ."

"Of course you are, Miss Foster. You're no old maid!"

"Stop that, Gerry," Claudia said, suppressing a laugh. "This is a man who is just beginning to study the Bible seriously. We need to pray that he'll accept truth."

\* \* \*

"You know, Mrs. Johnson," Lucky said as he stood up and collected his Bible and the papers Helen had given him, "you and your husband should take an offering when I come. You're doing a pastor's work without pay."

"Our pay is seeing you grow in the Lord, Lucky," Helen replied.

"But I'm certainly taking a lot of your time. Weeknights, weekends. I can't tell you how much I appreciate your help."

"Please don't mention it. We are the ones who are blessed."

"I can't get over how much I've learned these past two months."

"Of all the things you've studied during this time, what has been your greatest surprise so far, Lucky?"

"Surprise? You mean shock. Finding out that people who are really informed—pastors, theologians, churchmen—make no pretense that Sunday is Sabbath or that the change to Sunday is Biblical."

"That's right. Please sit down again, Lucky. It's not that late. Mark will miss seeing you if you leave before he gets back from visiting his mother in River Bend. Besides, there's something I meant to show you the other night when we talked about the change of Sabbath to Sunday."

Lucky waited expectantly. Helen went to the bookcase and pulled out a paperbound volume. "Notice the name of the publisher of this book."

*"The Question Box,"* Lucky read, taking the book from her.

"As you can see, it's a Catholic publication that gives answers to questions people ask about various beliefs of that church. I want you to read the questions and answers on pages 254 and 255."

Lucky found the pages and read three questions:

What does the Catholic Church say about Sunday as the Sabbath?

What Bible authority is there for changing the Sabbath from the seventh day to the first day of the week?

Who gave the pope authority to change a command of God?

"Now the answer," Helen said.

*Answer:* If the Bible is the only guide for the Christian, then the Seventh-day Adventist is right in observing Saturday with the Jew. But Catholics learn what to believe and do from the divine, infallible authority established by Jesus Christ, the Catholic Church, which in apostolic times made Sunday the day of rest to honor our Lord's resurrection on that day, and to mark off clearly the Jew from the Christian. . . . Is it not strange that those who make the Bible their only teacher should inconsistently follow in this matter the traditions of the church?

"You see," Helen laughed, "an Adventist has the sanction of the Catholic Church in keeping Saturday for Sabbath."

"Well, isn't that something!"

"One reason Adventists lay so much emphasis on the Sabbath—not that it is more imperative than the other nine commandments—is that it is the only one whose validity for today is challenged," she commented.

"Other than that, you wouldn't consider it special above the others?"

"It does have a special significance in drawing our attention back to the Creator God, as you will see as you continue to study it."

"Those nine First-day texts my pastor—my *former* pastor, I'd better call him now—showed me as evidence for Sundaykeeping the other night when he came to see me about my studying Adventist doctrines, not one of them attaches any sacredness to Sunday. I can see that now."

"I can even give you a quotation by the founder of your former church," Helen offered, savoring the full impact of Lucky's use of the word *former*, "Alexander Campbell. It refers to changing the Sabbath to Sunday 'by that august personage who changes times and laws *ex officio* . . . Dr. Antichrist.' His words, not mine!"

"I wonder if my mother and dad are aware of that?"

"Probably not. You will have to be very tactful about this. Longtime loyalty to a church is difficult to uproot. Don't expect a favorable reaction—at first, at least."

"I won't. I'm already getting hands-off signals from them." Lucky stood up. "This time I'm leaving for sure, Helen," he said, exercising the first-name privilege she had long since urged upon him.

He started out the door, then stopped and turned back. "What do you suppose Claudia would say if she knew I was going to keep my first Sabbath this week?"

\* \* \*

Helen's latest letter was lying on Claudia's desk when she came in from school. "Dear Claudia," she began, "Progress report on Lucky!"

Absorbed with the contents, she sat down on the bed. Outside her window the first robins were hopping about in the greening grass. A soft April breeze stirred the curtains. March had made a blustery exit a few days before, and a sudden burst of spring had stripped everyone of boots, coats, and mittens, liberating them from winter's prison. But of the bursting buds and singing birds, she was oblivious.

"He is now a Sabbathkeeper; isn't that *wonderful?* He asked his boss in the office at Founders Furnace—where he now works, did you know?—if he could put in extra time the other five days and have Saturday morning off. And you know, his boss said Yes, without any problem. Nothing like your Mr. Berry. Remember him?"

Although it was now seven years later, she remembered Mr. Berry, all right. If he only knew it, he had done her a favor. Had he not fired her she might never have gone to school. Why, she could still be pushing a billing machine around at Fidelity Bank and Trust in River Bend!

But the news about Lucky! Of all people, him keeping Sabbath. She could hardly picture it.

"Imagine Lucky," the letter went on, "walking down Front Street in Lakeville and into our church rooms above the village hall, carrying his Bible, waving to his friends on the way *(everybody* knows Lucky). 'Where you going, Lucky?' they ask, and he says unabashedly, 'To church. Today is

Sabbath.' What courage!

"Well, it's only a matter of time till he is baptized, I feel sure. He has studied and accepted most of the points of doctrine. Oh yes, I forgot to mention—he quit smoking some time ago. Just laid the habit aside completely—with divine help, naturally—when he started studying the Bible seriously.

"As for alcohol, I don't think that was ever really a problem, but about the time he quit smoking, he also announced, 'No more social drinks for me.' Then the other night it seemed the right time to proceed into the question of healthful living. He knew, of course, about Battle Creek and Kellogg's Corn Flakes and peanut butter and all, and he was interested in how Ellen White—whom I introduced along with this study—knew the principles of clean living and proper diet so far ahead of her time.

"He also wanted to know why this health message is such an integral part of Adventist doctrine. I explained our philosophy on the interrelationship of the three human components: mind, body, and spirit—head, heart, and hand, as we say. As a former athlete and ski trooper, Lucky needed little convincing. He just needed the whys.

"The other night he mentioned *you* for the first time in connection with our studies. 'What would Claudia think?' he asked. Well, what *do* you think? Let me know!—Love, Helen."

Claudia put down the letter and lay back on her bed. What did she think? Why, she couldn't believe it, really. It seemed improbable, *impossible*. Lucky actually accepting Adventist beliefs *after all these years*. "I think it's great, that's what I think!" she said aloud.

Then she sat bolt upright. Why not let Helen and Lucky know in person what she thought? With spring break coming up, why not head for Lakeville and give him her personal blessing!

* * *

"Dear Claudia," Helen's next letter began. "We're delighted you're going to spend your spring break with us!

## IN RETROSPECT: THE WAY IT ALL HAPPENED

Your 5:00 P.M. arrival time is written in red on the calendar. We're looking forward to seeing you after so long a time. Gladys and George are, too, and Jennifer has lots to tell you, not to mention the basketball exploits Eric is waiting to report. You won't believe how tall he is.

"Thanks for sending the carbon copy of the article you wrote, 'What's a Heaven For?' So you got $15 for it. Doesn't that make you a professional? My sister, the writer—imagine!

"We'll be on the alert for the issue of the *Signs of the Times* in which it appears. I can see it already, with the lines from Robert Browning you borrowed the title from, printed in italics above the article: 'Ah, but a man's reach should exceed his grasp/Or what's a heaven for?' With maybe a picture, an artist's conception, of heaven beside it, and of course the name of the author (ahem!).

"And speaking of borrowing—without asking your permission, but giving you full credit, I used that article as Lucky's Bible study on heaven and the new earth. It came at the very moment needed. Another of the Lord's providences. Isn't it gratifying to be used as His handmaiden?

"Lucky loved it. He left no doubt he wants to be there.—Love, Helen."

Claudia laid the letter on her desk. So Helen had shared it with him. To think that the Lord had used her own inadequate writing effort to teach him about the wonders of eternity. It was a subject she herself loved to dwell on. Opening a drawer, she got out her article and read again the last paragraph: "Joy and gladness, beauty and melody, refreshing work, fellowship with the saints of all ages, with the inhabitants of other worlds, and with God—these will be the portion of the redeemed in an earthly heaven, a heavenly earth. There it will be that 'the meek shall inherit the earth'; there will be answered the prayer 'Thy will be done on earth as it is in heaven'; there will a man's reach *meet* his grasp—it's what a heaven's for."

Oh, how I want to be there! Claudia thought. And she wondered, as she put the article away and opened the first in a stack of sophomore workbooks, if heaven had a tiny corner reserved for unemployed English teachers.

\* \* \*

The trip to Lakeville took Claudia through countryside burgeoning with spring, buds bursting, crocuses and daffodils nodding brightly. Rolling into town, the bus passed old familiar streets and houses that spoke almost audibly one name: Lucky.

It was his town, all right, and there stood the steepled white church he had so often tried to lure her into. She had not been any more successful in luring him—rather, bludgeoning him with doctrine—into her own church. Now it was surely the power of God's Spirit and the love of Jesus that were drawing him there.

A person had to be ready to listen to the Spirit, of that she was now convinced. He had not been ready in 1941—now in 1947, he was.

The hissing of air brakes ended her brown study abruptly. They were at the station. Which one would be meeting her, Helen or Mark? Today was Sunday. Mark would not be working. They'd both be there, no doubt.

As she stepped down from the bus, she saw that it was neither. Coming toward her, smiling broadly, was Lucky Marshall.

"Hello, Claudia," he said, taking her overnight bag. "Glad you decided to come to Lakeville for Easter."

"Hello, Lucky." For some reason she felt shy. Here was a man she had planned a long time ago to marry but had had to shut out of her heart. In the few times he had reappeared in her life in recent months, she had been able—with some effort—to remain aloof and objective. Under no circumstances would she have considered him for a marriage partner. From the beginning she had determined not to be "unequally yoked" with an unbeliever, even if he had asked her—which of course he hadn't. And even if she herself had then been free to accept—which of course she wasn't. So until now Lucky was someone to pray for, with a nagging disbelief that the prayers would ever have an answer.

Now he stood before her, still the charming person he had always been, all but an Adventist. And all the barriers removed, on *both* sides. Of course she was shy!

Reminding herself that if she was aware of their mutual eligibility, *he* was not, and suppressing her momentary discomposure, she smiled back. "It's nice to be in Lakeville, and nice of you to meet me, Lucky."

"Helen and Mark insisted, over my strong protests, of course."

"Well!" Claudia replied, mock injury in her tone. "I've had more willing chauffeurs in my time." She turned as if to go into the station.

Lucky took her arm and propelled her to the car, both laughing, her shyness disappearing. "Come on, as long as I've gone to all the effort, we may as well go through with it. Get in. I'll fetch your luggage." He returned with her bag, stowed it in the trunk, and got in beside her.

"I've heard that good things are happening in your life," Claudia volunteered as they started off.

"Good? That's an understatement. Marvelous things have been happening, Claudia. I'm a different man."

"Please introduce me to this man. I don't believe we've met."

"Well, the 'old man' is still there, of course. Wasn't it Paul who said that the 'old man' must die daily? But what I mean is that my life has changed. I'm going in a new direction—with the help of the Lord. So meet Andrew Marshall, newest recruit in the Lord's army!"

"I'm pleased to meet you, soldier." Tears welled up in her eyes.

"Did Helen tell you? I've been attending your church—our church, that is—the last two Sabbaths."

"She did. It seems like a miracle."

"It is a miracle. I only wish . . . it had happened years ago."

Claudia was silent a moment. It was not exactly a lead for explaining her new status. She was too shy at this point, too unsure that his remark reflected other than regret for years wasted without the Lord.

"We are all ready to listen to God's voice at different times in our life. My moment of readiness was not yours. I'm so pleased that when your moment arrived, you didn't let it slip by."

"Thanks for the encouragement. I'm counting on your prayers—as I did overseas in battle. I still have so much to learn, so far to go."

"Christian maturity is the work of a lifetime, Lucky."

They turned into the Johnsons' drive. "Here we are. Let me get the door for you." Lucky jumped out and reached her door in a moment. Together they went to the trunk to get her bags, chatting amiably.

From the window, Helen and Mark watched them approach the house.

"Oh, Mark, they make such a handsome couple. Roger is nice, but . . ."

"I feel that way too. But there's nothing we can do about it now."

"It's good that Lucky is so happy in Jesus—the 'first love' the Bible speaks of. He doesn't have much room in his heart for anything else. Have you noticed, all the while he has been studying, he's rarely mentioned Claudia, except to say something like 'Claudia told me that once,' or 'I know now what Claudia was talking about years ago'?"

The bell rang then, and the Johnsons welcomed Claudia with hugs and questions and comments on her newly acquired weight.

"Much, much better," Mark commented. "You were far too thin when you left college."

"Mrs. Landers has stuffed me like a goose. I hope I can take a vacation from eating this week."

"Not at all. We've got a good supper waiting in the oven right now," Helen said. "Lucky's staying too. This evening I promised to tell him about William Miller and the great Disappointment."

"I've been waiting for that story for a long time," he said.

Later at the supper table Claudia permitted herself to

enjoy Lucky's company as she had not in seven years. *Seven years!* Just as long as Jacob waited for Rachel. She wondered if Lucky realized that today was the seventeenth of April. Ever since 1940, that date had always stood out on her calendar as if printed in red, even in the years when the distance between them, both literally and figuratively, was vast, even in the year of Phil Gardner.

She wondered if she should remind Lucky what day it was, then immediately opted against it. The time was not ripe. So far, he had come step by step to Christ without any inkling that she was not still engaged. His recent decisions had had nothing to do with her. She had deliberately refrained from telling Helen and Mark about herself, lest Lucky should learn. It was gratifying to know that he was committing himself to the Lord and her church altogether on his own.

Until it seemed proper to make known her "spinster" status, she could relax meanwhile and enjoy being with him without the discomfort of feeling disloyal to someone else. She listened happily to his reaction to references to God's goodness, she watched appreciatively as he served himself a second portion of the vegetarian roast. Nor were his clean-cut good looks lost on her. Here was a real man of the world who was no longer *of* the world. It was impossible, it was wonderful!

The meal progressed at a leisurely pace, with each one contributing to the animated table talk. Mark spoke of his friend at work who kept trying to find proof in the Bible that people went straight to heaven when they died. Helen reported the activities of the Preston family next door. Lucky related several episodes that happened in his office, repeating for Claudia's benefit how he had arranged for Sabbath off. Claudia told about the bat in the study hall. They sat talking for some time after dessert, until Mark finally announced, "I am about to make an unprecedented offer."

"We await with bated breath," Helen replied.

"I propose to do KP while the rest of you adjourn to the

*salon,*" he said, pronouncing it *saloon.*

"What have we done to deserve this?" Claudia wanted to know.

"KP?" Lucky offered. "Better let an old infantryman help you out."

"Oh no," Mark insisted. "I want you to hear about William Miller."

"Then let us, by all means, repair to the drawing room," Helen said ceremoniously. The three of them carried their dishes to the sink and went into the living room.

"And now," said Lucky, "for the great Disappointment." They all laughed at the sound of it. Before long, however, Helen, with Claudia's help, was telling the serious story of William Miller and his followers.

"I'll look forward to the next study tomorrow night—if I may?" Lucky said sometime later. "Right now I must go. I don't want to keep you three up any longer, and I go to work at an unearthly hour in the morning—to make up Saturday time."

After they had said Good night to him and closed the door, Claudia stood looking out the window with a slight frown on her face. Helen lingered behind as Mark went off to bed.

"What's wrong, Claud? A disappointment of your own?"

Her sister wheeled around in surprise. "Why nothing's wrong . . . I mean . . . does it actually show?"

"Yes, it does. In fact, I got the feeling, as our discussion went on tonight, that you were somehow wishing we'd get it over with. I thought you'd enter more enthusiastically into Lucky's new experience."

"I'm thrilled about him, honest, Helen. If I'm disappointed tonight, it's because Lucky didn't say a word about looking forward to seeing *me* again, just to the next Bible lesson. Why, it was almost as if he didn't notice I was there."

"But isn't that a relief?" Helen said, a note of disapproval in her voice. "After all, you're engaged."

"After all, I'm *not* engaged. Not anymore, Helen."

The surprise that registered on Helen's face made

Claudia laugh.

"It's true," she insisted. "Roger and I broke up in February—before I ever knew Lucky had begun Bible studies."

"But you never said . . ."

"At first I didn't believe anything would come of it. O *me* of little faith! Then I held back because I didn't want my status to influence him in any way. I wanted him to accept truth because it was truth. I still don't want him to know. Not until his decision to join the church is signed and sealed."

"Claudia, Claudia, I am so happy. Not for Roger, of course, although I know he'll recover in time. I've never heard of anyone succumbing to heartbreak. But now, do you realize, if he . . . when he . . . you and Lucky . . ."

"I know, I know. And I hope . . . that is, do you think Lucky . . . could care for me again . . . ?"

In his room at home Lucky was just getting up from his bedside prayer. He had thanked God once again for giving him a second chance to learn Bible truth. His love for the Lord constantly grew as he studied the Scriptures further. And yet, as he lay in bed thinking over the evening, his mind turned to Claudia. In a way, it was better when she wasn't around. Even though she'd be in Lakeville only a few days, they would be days filled with remorse for him. If only he had had more sense when he was 20 and had listened to her then. Why, they could be long since married, maybe even parents by now. Still, it was no use thinking what might have been. He was sure that God was working all things together for good, and that he must look to the future instead of the past. But oh, if only she weren't engaged, how much he could care for her again . . .

\* \* \*

The next evening Claudia hurried through the supper dishes, took a shower, and dressed with care. Her salary did not accommodate many new clothes, but she had bought a dusty-rose spring suit. She put on the skirt with a frilly blouse to match, hoping to catch the eye of a certain serious Bible student about to ring the bell. Not that she intended for a moment to distract him from the evening's study, but if it happened afterward, well, that possibility was worth some extra fussing at the mirror. At last she felt satisfied with the reflection there. Although she had never laid claim to real beauty, she did not feel exactly plain, and tonight she saw an attractive color in her cheeks, heightened by anticipation—and a coppery shine in her shoulder-length hair. All in all, she felt quite presentable.

Then she stationed herself in a chair near the window with a book in hand, which anyone passing by could have told her was upside down, but as she made little pretense of reading, she didn't notice. It wasn't long until she saw in the spring twilight the tall figure of Lucky coming down the street. Soon he stood waiting at the door. A lock of his wavy black hair had blown onto his forehead. Unsuccessfully he tried to smooth it back as he greeted her. He was wearing a blue cardigan, with open shirt collar, sharply creased gray slacks, shoes polished to rigid army standards. Somehow he looked even handsomer, Claudia thought, than he had the previous night.

When he was seated inside, she called Helen. "Hello, Lucky," Helen said, entering the room. "I think we'll start without Mark. He's helping George with an emergency plumbing job."

Lucky opened the discussion. "I've been reading about the tabernacle in my Old Testament study. Did William Miller ever learn the truth about 1844?"

"No, he died in disappointment. But one day when the Lord comes, won't he have a delightful surprise?" Helen suggested.

"And," added Claudia, "plenty of time to study the 2300 days!"

"I'm certainly impressed how the Lord has led the church through the ages step by step right up to now. What surprises me is how few people study these prophecies, how the ministers in the pulpit ignore them. I certainly want to do my share to let people know, beginning with my family."

"We all feel that way," Claudia added.

## IN RETROSPECT: THE WAY IT ALL HAPPENED

To herself she said, "I hope your family is more receptive than mine." Ever since her baptism she had still not been invited home. She had written through the years, and occasionally her mother would respond, never her father. She sighed as she thought of the great disappointment in her own life.

For the next hour and a half Helen and Claudia led Lucky through the various prophetic periods of the 2300 days. As they finished the lesson, he said, "I'll have to give you time off now, Helen, while I catch up in my personal study—especially this diagram you gave me showing the various divisions of the 2300 days. I won't be back till the weekend, probably." He stood up to leave. "Thanks again. Say Hello to the plumber for me."

As he opened the door, he paused, then turned to Claudia. "Will I see you again, Claudia, before you go back to school?"

"Oh, I *hope* so," she said.

Lucky gave her a quick look. Her voice had more enthusiasm in it than he had a right to expect.

"I'm leaving Thursday afternoon," she went on. "I need to get back before the weekend and plan my lessons. School is on again at seven-thirty Monday morning, I'm afraid." She paused. It was time to take some kind of action. Lucky was almost out of the door. "Can you come back Wednesday evening for a while?"

"I'm here so often my folks think I may as well move in."

"Please do come," Helen said, realizing he was waiting for her approval. "For supper, why not? Mark and I have an appointment that evening afterward."

"We do?" Mark asked, coming in the door just then. Then noticing Helen's slight, encouraging nod, he added, "Oh, that's right, we do. So come to supper, Lucky, by all means."

"I'll be here promptly at six," he promised. As he walked to his home not many blocks away, his step had a certain spring to it. For some reason, he had a premonition of pleasure, not necessarily implied by a mere supper invitation, as good a cook as Helen was.

\* \* \*

The talk at the supper table that Wednesday evening lingered on after the meal. Mark and Lucky had begun trading Army experiences, and Claudia thought they would never stop. She kept giving her brother-in-law signals, periodically trading surreptitious glances with Helen. Finally Mrs. Johnson stood up.

"You two can talk war another time. We're going to be late, Mark."

"Claudia and I will do the dishes," Lucky offered. "Don't be late for your appointment."

Helen laughed to herself. She hoped Lucky wouldn't follow them to the door and see them take the path to the Preston house next door. An appointment indeed! But she hadn't actually stretched the truth—they had a *standing* appointment for a visit with Gladys and George any time!

"Thanks, Lucky," Mark said. "I wasn't planning to be as magnanimous as I was the other night. There were more dishes than I bargained for!"

Lucky did not follow them to the door. Instead, he went to the sink and began running hot water into the dishpan.

"I'll wash and you dry," Claudia said, gently pushing him away.

"Just like the good old days, right?"

He took a dish towel. Neither spoke as they began to work. He wished he hadn't made the remark about the good old days. It brought back too many memories and made him feel a little tongue-tied. When Mark and Helen were with them, it was easier to be casual with Claudia.

"Speaking of the good old days," she said, ending the long pause, "had you noticed what date it was Sunday when you met me at the bus?"

The dish Lucky was drying was already polished to a high sheen, but he kept rubbing it industriously. "I never forget that date, Claud. I thought you probably had, so I didn't mention it."

Another pause. Her mind was in a whirl. This seemed

such a good lead. Why couldn't she follow up? Why couldn't she ask him outright if he was definitely going to join the church, and if so, was he interested in one of its single members? Patience, Claudia, she told herself, in the Lord's own time things will work out if they are supposed to. Don't run ahead of Him.

"Lucky," she said aloud. "I've been wondering, now that you've committed your life to Jesus, if you've ever felt impressed to become a minister?"

"Oh yes, I have. I definitely want to go back to college and then into the Lord's work someday."

As they finished the dishes, they discussed his plans, what courses he would study, how long it would take. Talk flowed smoothly, on a much more comfortable level than when the "good old days" and the seventeenth of April had come up. Dishes done, they went into the living room and sat down together on the sofa.

"Would you go to an Adventist college?" she couldn't resist asking.

"Definitely. Haven't I made myself clear? Why, I'm going to be baptized just as soon as Helen has finished my lessons and she thinks I'm ready for heaven."

She savored his words silently for a minute. He had said it, she had heard him. Lucky was actually going to join the church—why, he was already virtually an Adventist. Her heart began to sing and her voice longed to join. Controlling her emotions, she said, "You were ready for the kingdom the moment you gave your heart to the Lord. And so long as you continue to *want* to do His will, even when you fail, you are ready. It's the intent and motives of the heart that count, Lucky. Our actions sometimes betray us."

"The 'old man' isn't quite dead at those times, is he?"

"The old *maid* in my case," Claudia said, laughing as she thought of how she had called herself that to Gerry.

"You, an old maid? That's a good one, Claud. You and Roger will soon be going down the center aisle, won't you?"

"No, we won't, Lucky." She paused to let the full effect of her words reflect in his astonished eyes. "You see, Roger and

I are no longer engaged."

\* \* \*

It was seven-ten Monday morning. As Claudia hurried to class, the day was already balmy and bright with spring sunshine, just made for lingering along the way, to shake off winter's remaining cobwebs. But such luxury was not for her this morning. She had only a few minutes to get ready to teach her seven-thirty class. She would have to play it by ear all day. Did *experienced* teachers ever do this? Would the conference "sup" pop in on her at this unprepared moment? She fervently hoped not.

But she had nobody but herself to blame that she had made no lesson plans. Herself and Lucky, on second thought. He had persuaded her to stay till Sunday when he could drive her back to Broadvale. They had been together on Thursday evening and Friday evening, and they had gone to church together the next day in Lakeville.

Lucky seemed to know the answers even better than most of the members of the class they attended in Sabbath school. Nor did he seem at all hesitant about attending what a few years back he would have called a "storefront" church. She was glad he had heard the pastor speak of future plans to build a new church.

Elder and Mrs. Landers had been well impressed with Lucky, too. They had invited him to stay for supper, and he had had a sample of Mrs. Landers' pie. "A real Christian gentleman," Pastor Landers called him later.

As Claudia arrived on campus, she saw heading toward the ad building an early bird, her loyal friend Gerry, no doubt getting there early to catch up on the news and to report her own. Now how to find time to steal a glance at the lesson she had to teach in a few minutes? Oh well, Claudia told herself, she'd manage somehow. "Gerry," she called, "wait!"

The girl stopped and turned around. "Why, Miss Foster, you sounded so young, I thought it was my roommate calling me."

"Well, I'm not quite as old as this building, for instance," she said, as they walked past the 1898 cornerstone and into the door.

"So don't call yourself an old maid, then," Gerry teased. "Isn't it a *glorious* day?"

"It certainly is, positively glorious." Then suspecting her student had a reason for her choice of adjective, she added, "Is it, for some reason, especially so for you?"

"Yes, ma'am! Johnny and I have made up. We're going to the girls' reception together. I asked him."

"Shocking! You know, don't you, that the boy is supposed to chase the girl until she finally catches him!"

"You and your funny sayings, Miss Foster."

They entered the classroom and put down their books. Claudia began to arrange her things on her desk, and Gerry strolled to the bulletin board. The Week of Prayer display was still there. She began to read offhandedly, "Prayer is the key in the hand of faith . . ."

"Gerry," Claudia said, "you remember the man our prayer band was praying for, especially during prayer week?"

"The one you said your sister was studying with? His name was Andrew Marshall, I think."

"Yes, that's the one. Well, there's good news. He's going to be baptized next month."

"True?" The girl's 16-year-old enthusiasm immediately bubbled forth. "Oh, Miss Foster, that's just wonderful. Our prayers have been answered. That's just *super.*"

Claudia could no longer contain herself.

"That's not all, Gerry."

"No? What else?"

"Andrew Marshall and I are going to be married in June."

"Miss Foster! Oh, Miss *Foster!*" Then she turned on her heel and ran out to tell the world.

# Epilogue

Lucky and Claudia were married June 14, 1947, and since then have been living happily ever after—not exactly as in the storybooks, but certainly with just as much adventure. Together they served their church for a combined total of 52 years, 11 of them as missionaries in Africa. Their two grown children, a son and a daughter, along with a son-in-law, share their love for God and His Seventh-day Adventist Church and also work for the church.